Holding A Séance By Myself

Thomas Townsley

Standing Stone Books
Fabius, New York

Holding a Séance By Myself

First printing, 2020

Reproduction without express permission from the author or publisher is prohibited.

Standing Stone Books is a subsidiary of Standing Stone Studios, an organization dedicated to the promotion of the literary and visual arts.

Mailing address: 1897 State Route 91, Fabius, New York, 13063, USA
Email: standingstonebooks@gmail.com
web: www.standingstonebooks.net

This book is printed by Bookmobile, Minneapolis, Minnesota, and distributed by Small Press Distribution, Berkeley, California.

ISBN: 978-1-63625-648-1

Library of Congress Control Number: 2020945126

Book Design: Adam Rozum

Standing Stone Books is a member of the Community of Literary Magazines and Presses.

Acknowledgments

"Retroussé"" originally appeared in
Doubly Mad: An Independent Journal of Arts and Ideas.

Praise for "Holding A Séance By Myself"

Thomas Townsley still has a restless imagination. I say this as someone who has known him for over 40 years. What surprises me is how, in a work that invokes ghosts from the past, in a mode of retrospection, he can't stop inventing.

Maybe that's because the ghosts keep surprising him. "There are ghosts who do nothing but climb into your words. It's surprising the way they appear out of nowhere, ready to speak for you."

As a testament to his restlessness, this book has 333 questions. "Excuse me, is this the road to the necropolis? ...is there a kind of darkness that smothers sound? ...Do you know that the catbird mimics and rearranges the songs of other birds into a longer song of its own?"

I'm not sure he answers any of them. Sometimes he ponders what era we're in and what's to come. "I was searching in the closet for my missing Zeitgeist," he says, "in an age that no longer believes in epics and that sees the 'lyrical I' shattering into fragments."

I'm not sure if we've given up on "the lyrical I"—but perhaps the old genres never really die. Out of the fragments he melds animal fables, parables, liturgies, ghost stories, dream visions, political debates, a séance or two, or that ancient reminiscence called *ubi sunt*, Latin for "Where Are They Now?" so lately popular in the medieval era.

He seems to doubt originality, but I'm not sure he says this. "Was this, at last, the New Poem? .... Will corporate barons invent new forms of confetti?" Sometimes he might despair at finding the audience he deserves:

> She also told me there are pages written that go unread—and that's
> what I was next, an unread page, and that's what I remained for a long,
> long time, until you dog-eared me, and then I was a night of crickets singing,
> and then, just for a moment, I was you, turning the page—
> and then I was something burning.

Even so, he keeps inventing, perhaps because "things keep changing. Already the sky is afflicted / with mourning doves, each bearing in its beak an equal sign/ where the olive branch should be."

– Ron Block, author of *Dismal River* and *The Dirty Shame Motel*
(New Rivers Press)

Thomas Townsley, when he writes, is preaching the blues. "I keep your ghost in the closet to remind me of when I was alive," he says. "It's easier than calling you on the phone." But in these poems "a Bach fugue and a Robert Johnson song play simultaneously," and the narrator reminds us that we only see things as we do because we have "entered an Era of Sharp Distinctions within a Blurred Ideological Framework." In *Holding a Séance by Myself,* Townsley is up for anything, folk tale or lyric, slice of life, or danse macabre. Humor, in such a case, will not mollify the trouble, but the poet's combination of wit and misery does make a story worth telling: "Is it unfair to expect of mourning doves / more than three sad answers to the same question? // That is what I was thinking as my enthusiasm / for anarchy waned. I needed a career." Alert, skeptical, weary, fascinated with strangeness, he writes like Groucho under the influence of Apollinaire. Reading him is a dark pleasure.

– Brroks Haxton, author of *Fading Hearts on the River,* the true story of his son's career in high-stakes poker, and *Mister Toebones,* a collection of poems forthcoming in February 2021.

"I push words in wheelbarrows no one depends on," quips the narrator of one of the poems in Thomas Townsley's *Holding a Séance by Myself.* But I beg to differ. This collection is a darkly humorous delight—a place where your cocktail will take a week to mix, where a medieval theologian narrates your naughty dreams, and where the safe word is—literally—"literally." Like the best absurdism, though, there's a swift undercurrent of seriousness in his play. "How many ways exist to gild the darkness?" asks one poem, whose narrator claims to know of seven. Townsley clearly knows hundreds upon hundreds, each one more dazzling than the last.

– Philip Memmer, author of *Pantheon*

This book is dedicated to my children, Robert and Jennifer
And to the members of The Scotch Committee
Lang may yer lum reek.

Table of Contents

First Session

Second Session

Third Session

Fourth Session

First Session

The Curfew

The Civic Improvement Committee chopped down all the trees. Then they held a parade on Main Street to honor them. Float after float passed by: oak, maple, poplar, mountain ash, all neatly chopped and stacked. All the leaves burned in barrels.

It was an anemic spring day, so the whole town turned out. Even the previous night's moon pressed its back to the sky and refused to budge until the festivities ended. "Probably drunk," some members of The Moral Improvement Committee were heard to whisper.

After the parade, I returned home—well before the curfew. I went into the study and saw that my dead uncle was back. He was sitting behind my desk, playing with the snow globe.

"Now what?" I said.

My dead uncle set the snow globe down and drummed his gray fingers on the desktop. "It was just after the war," he said. "I could finally quit seminary. I met June and your mother at the Victory Parade."

"How long is this going to take?" I asked.

For some reason unknown to me, my dead uncle had begun to appear nightly in order to tell me his life story. I'd listened politely to the first few installments, but after several weeks he'd grown tedious—three days just for the school years! What's more, his stories always took strange turns, became fantastical and discontinuous. It took me awhile to understand that the dead are always dreaming—that ghosts are, in effect, dreams of themselves—and therefore they find mimesis difficult, dramatic unity nearly impossible.

"I am of sanguine humor," he shouted. "How am I supposed to know how long it will take? Time is elastic, anyway. Now where was I?"

"You were on your deathbed," I said.

My dead uncle fixed me in his ashen gaze. I could tell he was angry. "Do you know what you are?" he hissed. He rose slowly—and he kept rising until his head touched the ceiling. He'd never been that tall in life. "A melancholic," he said. "You and your whole damned family."

"Then why don't you go away?" I replied. "I don't understand why you're appearing to me in the first place. You're not my real uncle. You just married my mother's best friend. You have five children of your own."

"What do you mean *I'm* appearing to *you*?" He leaned closer till I could smell the grave. "*You're* appearing to *me*!" he exclaimed.

"I don't have time for your nonsense," I said. "It's almost curfew."

And it was! I knew I had to hurry! I ran to the closet and checked for cats. All clear. Next, I went from room to room, drawing the curtains—but leaving them open just a crack in case the Night Improvement Committee wanted to peer inside. Finally, with no time to spare—the sun was already down-- I dipped a brush in the pupil of my eye and began to paint the evening shadows on the wall.

The Spirit of the Age

We'd been one too many times to the well.
Our words seemed covered with a fine layer of fur.
This made communication warm but difficult.
We listened to the dog cough and watched the sunset
through many windows. You made a decent
living selling shade. I watched you counting
coins on a salver. The radio was tuned
to a magic show, or, rather, the narrative
of a magic show: "He passes a hoop over
the floating girl's body," the announcer was saying.
 "Why do you think they always put the levitating woman
in a trance first?" I asked. "I'll show you later," you replied,
letting another coin drop. That was the year we first noticed
a shortage of catbirds. That was the year I carried an
imaginary lariat. All the stations cancelled their weather reports.
You packed a suitcase that was not imaginary,
then unpacked it, each and every day. Gradually,
we forgot all the Morse code we ever knew, but this
opened the way to a more complicated, more secretive
means of communication. Some of it involved feathers and twine.
Some of it involved quotes by William Hazlitt. "'The most
insignificant people are the most apt to sneer at others,'" you said.
"Why is it always a rabbit?" I replied. "Why is it always a hat?"
We both turned to gaze at the sandy bed where the marigolds once grew.
A spider began to build a web between us, beginning at the eyelids.
A few of your shadows slipped out the back door while you weren't looking.
"Do you think that likening Gideon's trumpet to a man-made
brass instrument sort of undersells it?" I asked. You stopped
counting. You looked at me and smiled. The dog coughed again.
The nothingness between us sparkled like ions before a storm.
We'd both felt like this before, though what that feeling was,
neither could say.

Happy Hour

The White Stag stumbles out of the underbrush, looking muddy and burr-covered and generally non-mythological, but its eyes beckon, so I follow it anyway, over candy wrappers and discarded vestments, into a corner tavern. As my eyes adjust to the music, I observe that the place is nearly empty, except for a nineteenth century circus strongman—bald, waxed moustache, striped muscle shirt—sitting in the corner booth, reading Nietzsche's *Genealogy of Morals*. "Now there's a conversation to avoid," I tell myself; I've learned from bitter experience not to interrupt men mired in philosophy.

"That would be like trout fishing on the Ganges," says the bartender, appearing out of nowhere.

His response catches me off guard. Was I thinking aloud again? The last time I did that, vestments were discarded. Small, gray birds befriended me. Clouds of gnats held up traffic for days.

"What'll it be?" the bartender asks. I take my place on the barstool of beatitude, and ponder my thirst. Is it a clowns-in-a-phone-booth or a sorrow-of-sparrows quenching that I need? The clock on the wall has ideas of its own; the second hand rotates in reverse, like a whirlpool south of the equator. It's tiring, occupying space and time simultaneously, I think to myself.

"And the Ganges is gray with ashes," says the bartender.

I don't want to keep him waiting, so I order a Supernal Chalice Buster, straight up. "And make it a double, my good man."

"That'll take me a week to mix," says the bartender.

"I can wait," I say. I look up and see The White Stag nodding in approval. On its antlers, tiny points of light blink on and off, like new and ever-changing constellations of preferable worlds.

Retroussé

I was tuned between stations, not even
thinking of you. A subliminal hum snuck up,
disguised as longing. "They don't make that
in my size," I bellowed—then I retreated to a
place of greater buoyancy. A distant clock
chimed the hours, each tone forming concentric rings
in whatever I was floating in. Before I knew it,
someone whispered "Turn your hymnals to page 188."
Was it you? It didn't sound like something you'd say,
nor did it sound like your voice. Still, I couldn't be sure.
It was like a dream in which you see someone and
know who it is, but they look nothing like that person
in the waking world. Maybe the hair's the wrong color,
or they're too tall, or their nose doesn't look right, like, it's not—
what's that word for "turned up at the end"? Anyway,
it didn't sound like you, and soon we were singing
"Faith of Our Fathers." Then something flew past my
peripheral vision, and the preacher mentioned The Story
of the Loaves and Red Herrings; then the walls fell away,
and our pew was floating toward a great cataract.
Everything took on an incredible clarity. My senses felt
truly anchored: emerald gliding water. Foam and rainbow.
It was a clarity for which no words were needed. It spelled
the end of narrative, but only briefly. The edge approached,
as edges must. I saw the jagged rocks below—the black teeth
of negation, and then the subliminal hum returned, and then
my brain shuffled its deck, and the card I drew was you.

Weltanschauung

That was the year we wore yellow scarves. That was the year the sun dogs went away. I remember we lived in a valley between blue hills. We lived there in the loosest sense of the word "lived."

I remember oat fields shimmering in the heat. God was a kindly German grandfather who mowed his lawn twice a week. Also, I remember the assembly line workers went on strike, though what they assembled escapes me.

You were there, but your lips are sealed, or were. It's not clear whether you are still with me. It's not clear what is then and what was now.

If I recall, we dwelled in a transitional era between honest craftsmanship and mass manufacture—of *what* escapes me.

That was the year before The Decree.

That was the year before we hung the street signs.

That was the year we imagined our own funerals for the first time.

Everyone was coming of age.

All of us attended the ribbon cutting ceremony.

That was the year three-part harmony was almost invented, and we got to choose what color the flowers would be.

Of course, it wasn't long before discarded yellow scarves began to litter the roadside, tossed from speeding station wagons. Clearly their fashionable days were coming to an end.

Some of us considered parades self-aggrandizing, while others did not. I can't remember your opinion on the subject, or whether you favored clemency or police brutality for the strikers.

We had brutality in abundance of course. Some of us are still bleeding. In retrospect, it's clear some of us were asking for too much.

Drinking From The Garden Hose, Metaphysically Speaking

"There are certain ratios of waist to hip, certain angles of jaw and clavicle, known to induce spiritual ache in aesthetically sensitive persons," said the man at the bar.

I looked up from my beer. I hadn't seen the man come in. There were no other customers—just Theo, the bartender, rinsing glasses at the far end of the room. Patsy Cline's voice hang-glided from the jukebox.

"Excuse me?" I said.

"I, myself, am a living Golden Mean," the man said. He was seated three stools down, with his back half turned. "Many women see me and feel a burning deep inside. Many men, too. I have that effect."

"You mean the way an onion makes your eyes burn?" I asked. Daddy always said if you're going to pick a fight, you may as well pick one with an aesthete.

"If you'd seen the Elgin Marbles, you'd know what I'm talking about," the man said. He still hadn't turned to face me—as if I wasn't worth the effort. "The Greeks made a study of aesthetics. They discovered the rules of just proportion."

"Fuck just proportion, and fuck the Elgin Marbles," I said. "Bunch of broken stones. And guess what? I'm glad they're broken! What do you think of that?"

The man said nothing.

"The problem with people like you," I went on, "is that you think beauty can be reduced to mathematics."

The man sighed and shook his head. "Friend," he said, "you're confusing reduction and distillation. Remember that the most beautiful music is still mathematics—pitch, frequency, duration, volume—all numbers. Yet that fact doesn't 'reduce' anything. Mathematics is a distilled language. It brings us closer to the ideal harmony."

"Broken stones!" I shouted. "Their missing limbs, their imperfections, their gaps and finitude—these invoke a poignancy your numerical formulae can't touch!" I stopped for a moment. Why was I talking like this? I really had no idea of what I was saying, but I was on a roll, so I went on. "Beauty exists only on the cusp of mortality. It's fleeting, and we know it. That's what moves us, you stupid bastard." I stood up and waited.

"You really are confused," the man said. "Poignancy and beauty are not synonymous. Beauty is eternal. It partakes of the divine light."

"Come over here and say that!" I shouted. I raised my fists.

"Very well," the man said. He slowly swiveled on his barstool to face me.

My eyes widened. My fists unclenched. It was like someone opened a door to the closet of my brain and let the light in. Patsy Cline's voice became angels singing the square root of primary numbers all along my spine. My weight, my physical bulk, seemed to drift away in eddies. Currents passed through me—or I was a current passing through something else—except "something else" was the wrong term—I was a term—I was a terminal—I couldn't step in the same me twice.

When I came to, I was lying on my back. Through the fog, I saw Theo hovering over me. "Pops, are you alright?" he said.

"What happened?" I said. My voice felt strange, like an animal in a cave, like it wasn't really mine.

"You took quite a spill," Theo said.

I sat up. The room was spinning. "Where's that other guy?" I asked. "The one who was just here?"

"What other guy?" Theo said.

"He was sitting right over there." I pointed to the empty barstool. "You couldn't have missed him. He was the most beautiful man I've ever seen."

Theo regarded me quizzically. "Sorry, Pops. I never saw no other guy. You must've been dreaming." He smiled and winked. "Besides, this ain't that kind of bar," he said.

Reprieve for Imperild Gazelles

Someone beheaded the liturgist before our ceremony could begin.
His head rolled all the way to the third pew. We had acrimony in
abundance then. Without realizing it, we'd entered an Era of Sharp
tinctions within a Blurred Ideological Framework. Blood-lines mattered
once more—not the news I wanted to hear—and feudal weddings
thrived like deer ticks. Our picnic by the moat offered a brief respite,
but the serenity was broken by all those Ophelias floating by, singing
bawdy ditties out of tune. We wandered over the hill, hand in hand,
till we reached the meadow where the King's gazelles did gambol
(the word "cavort" being banished.) When you told me you'd forgotten
the wolf costumes, I felt the beach ball of our passion deflating then and there.
I left in a huff and a puff. A flock of dour magpies blocked the sun.
Malodorous breezes swept across the heath, dropping spit-bugs in my hair.
There came a sound of hooves. Then, like a wave of nostalgia, The King's
messenger appeared, bearing in his hand a royal document. "You've been
proclaimed His Lordship's Liturgist," he said. "His Majesty commands you
to write the official prayer book for our new religion." "Another one?" I said.
"Yes," said the messenger. "This one involves silk cloaks, astrolabes and
malefaction. Everything is to be painted periwinkle blue. Daguerreotypes are
forbidden. All citizens are required to carry tongs." "In that case, to Whom
are we praying?" I asked. "Is it the Almighty Lancer of Boils, the Tangler of Kites,
the Weaver of Penumbras, the Confounder of Translucency, or the Crop Duster
of the Seven Shades of Indifference?" The messenger consulted his scroll.
"It says here we shall pray to the Fissure of Memories Forged in False Fire," he
said. "That's a tough one," I replied, but suddenly it no longer mattered because
at that precise moment we entered The Era of Discordant Lexicons,
and, with my tongue disguised as a gravedigger, I made good my escape.

Some Thoughts Leave a Ring

Is it unfair to expect of mourning doves
more than three sad answers to the same question?

That is what I was thinking as my enthusiasm
for anarchy waned. I needed a career.

This meant I had to make and keep promises,
which I was loathe to do. Should I

wander the Alps with a French horn, starting avalanches?
Install grenade pins in household appliances?

Should I paint the shadows cast by equal signs
the way Constable painted clouds?

I had no musical, technical, nor artistic skills
—"proclivities" as Auntie Hecuba called them.

Besides, painting shadows required knowledge of fractal geometry,
and that seemed a slippery slope back to anarchy.

Ah, why are there so many parentheses within perception?
Why are there so many synapses to cross?

Naturally, I got a job teaching Rhetoric.
I bought a new suit, red shoes, a squirting boutonniere.

I walked into class Day One and said "Before my first cup
of coffee, I'm a masochist. After that, all bets are off."

The students yawned and went back to their phones.
"Someone stole the red herrings I'd saved for breakfast," I said.

"Does that make my words more or less true?"
"It makes me more or less not care," said a freckled kid

In the front row. I was glad I'd bought the boutonniere.
But it was clear my pedagogy fell on deaf ears—

not the least of which were my own. I applied
for a job in Administration. Still no word, so I wait.

As it turns out, biding time comes naturally to me.
I take a white pill in the morning and a pink pill at night.

At least I think I do. The doctor says not to mix them up,
or I'll have bad dreams. Meanwhile, I gaze out the window.

Shall I describe the color of the sky? Oyster shell gray?
A stone tablet in the rain? A mirror's back?

Or is it the color of laughter of One who does not get the joke?
Whatever it is, I wear that color like camouflage, or a shroud.

And so I wait. The phone is about to ring any moment.
Or perhaps it has already rung—or is ringing, even now.

I shore this moment against anarchy by clinging to it.
But things keep changing. Already the sky is afflicted

with mourning doves, each bearing in its beak an equal sign
where the olive branch should be.

A Quiver's Worth of Orphaned Hypotheses

Say "The sumac is bleeding!" or say "The dirigibles are coming!"
It's all the same thing. Welcome to The Age of Indeterminacy, in
whose fetid light we pray. Your bone-flowers and livid skeletons,
your frost–choked hibiscus, and your epistemological necessity
can't help you here. And once the mirrors go on strike, self-knowledge
is left to flounder in the *au jus* of dreams. These come in several
flavors, all written on the dew of a leaf: "familial," "Rotarian,"
"viscous," "self-flagellating," and "wet suit spelunking" are but a few.
If I had to eat a hat, I'd choose a pork pie. This, of course, is neither here
nor elsewhere. Forgive me. The point is, I've come this far without
mentioning bladderwort. Now that our soldiers have given up the ghost,
we are entering a Re-Enlightened Age, wherein all of us are busy
cleaning out glove boxes and throwing away proof of insurance.
And isn't it natural to think that "glove box" is an anachronistic
and perhaps even inaccurate term? Committees will surely be appointed
to draft a new name; likely candidates are "front trunk" and
"thingy space." Clearly, someone has been cherry-picking our
best ideas. Well, peace be unto them. Let turning leaves usher in
the boredom of a new dawn—yes, even newer than the last. When you
get right down to it, Time is humdrum, and memory's an infected follicle.
Like Father used to say, "What we are circling may be the drain, but
it might be a monk on holiday, rhetorically speaking." Good old Father!
He's polished off the unicycle and gone to town for cigarettes.
Mother just smiles and eats a glazed donut. Her forefinger circles her
right ear—is she making the crazy sign or brushing away a mosquito?
Either way, it's time to select our national cheese. I nominate Gruyere.

Telekinesis In A Minor Mode

I found it best to look sideways. Peripheral vision had more content to reveal. Peripheral hearing, too. I preferred to open random windows. I liked lucky accidents and seeming abstraction. Landscape painting was not my forte. Choosing a motif brought with it nearly insurmountable difficulties, not to mention tinnitus, tuned to the key of D—the same key dogs howl in, according to a shaman friend of mine. If that's true, think of the ramifications. Think of the marketing potential. I won't, because I block those things mentally. When I feel something, it's like turning a Hindemith sonata inside out and catching medicine balls on my chest. (Hippocrates was said to have invented medicine balls for his patients' therapy. I just fall in love.) I prefer psychosomatic illnesses to real ones, but not by much. I can't stop these black flowers from blooming. Maybe if I open this window I'll get the cross-ventilation I need. Maybe if I regard you with a series of glimpses, instead of the steady stare I think I want—you will be my landscape. After all, who wouldn't lie down in a field of crown vetch if Monet painted it? Some called him a "dabbler," but that was his *technique*. He had a heart like a bow-sprit. I'm more like poor Vincent, who couldn't hold the stars still. Every moment for us is like window blinds snapping open. And then there's the poet who lives beneath a toadstool. He sends me messages. No one has seen him, but we all pay homage—even though I prefer obsequies. Here is one message he sent me: "How many ways exist to gild the darkness? I personally know of seven. One is to live on a diet of scorched earth. One is to pretend dust motes are angels. One is to forget what everything means. One is to assign meaning to everything. One is to carry your furniture on your back. One is to practice writing ransom notes. And one must never be spoken, must remain a secret, like a cricket chirping inside a box in the belly of a beast caught in the teeth of some half-invented, half-forgotten god."

Drinking With Emma Brummel

Emma Brummel and I were entertaining a serious debate regarding recent trends in literature. I don't remember how it started, but I know brown liquor was involved. We sat in her apartment, swirling our drinks and making predictable assertions, or so it would seem.

The poetry of today, with its self-reflexive ironies, is a shallow trough," Emma Brummel said.

"'Shallow' as opposed to what?" I countered, pouring myself another drink. When she extended her glass, I poured one for her as well.

"I see what you're trying to do," Emma Brummel said. "If I say 'Shallow as opposed to deep,' you'll explain to me that 'depth' is a problematic metaphor, a metaphysical pipe-dream. You'll say that we all live on a slippery metonymic slope and that everything's a language game. You'll say that self-reflexive irony is necessary in an age that no longer believes in epics and that sees the 'lyrical I' shattering into fragments."

"I might question the use of spatial metaphors in general," I said. "But eventually that argument would become tired, and to that extent, you are right. So let's change the subject. Do you remember how we met?"

"Oddly, no," Emma Brummel said, draining her glass and once more extending it toward me. I refilled it.

"It was in a dream," I explained. "Maybe even this one. It's hard to tell, given the way time stretches and compresses." I refilled my glass also. "Anyway, in the dream, I was revisiting the old apartment building I lived in thirty-five years ago when I was in grad school: Falcon Heights, a big yellow brick monstrosity on the bad edge of town. I'd once watched a woman die of a heart attack in the lobby there as the medics tried to revive her. I'd spoken to her a few times previously. Nice lady, though with a bit of that neurotic weirdness that living alone in such a place inevitably induces. But in the dream, the lobby had been remodeled into a sort of gift shop. Lots of glass trinkets in glass cases, as I recall. Also, there was a concierge stationed there who doubled as a cashier.

"Hans," Emma Brummel said.

"So that's his name?" I replied, pouring us each a stiff one. "Good to know."

"Do go on with your narrative," Emma Brummel said. "Get to the part where we meet. Try to use colorful description."

"Very well. So I was nosing about in the gift shop, feeling a backwash of nostalgia, when the concierge—"

"Hans," Emma Brummel reminded me.

"—when *Hans* noticed me dawdling. He asked 'Can I help you?' in a rather imposing manner, as if he sensed I didn't belong there—like I was looking to steal one of his trinkets. Or worse."

"Hans can be brusque," Emma Brummel said.

"Right. And his question caught me off guard, snapped me out of my reverie, so to speak. And then I suddenly felt somewhat embarrassed for being there. I'd just stopped by to revisit an old haunt, to stir up old memories. But rather than explain this, which would have taken several minutes to convey in the necessary detail, with proper nuance, so that he would understand and even empathize with my motives, I said 'I'm looking for someone named Emma. Does she still live here?' Now mind you, I'm just making this up on the fly, trying to save face. I didn't know anyone named Emma in those days."

"Interesting," Emma Brummel said. "Pour me another."

I did. Myself, too.

"What happened next?" Emma Brummel asked.

"Well, of course Hans said 'What's her last name?' I felt a bit on the spot, as you might imagine, but I figured I could make up a name—any name--, and when Hans told me no such person lived here, I could save face by saying 'Oh, she must have moved' or 'I must have the wrong address.' So I said 'Brummel.' The name came strictly out of the blue. I don't know anyone named Brummel. I don't recollect ever meeting anyone with that name, though of course it may be possible. But I've since thought about it, and I really don't remember such a person."

"Isn't that funny!" Emma Brummel said.

"Indeed! So you can imagine my surprise when Hans said 'Allow me to ring her up for you.'"

"I'm trying to do just that," Emma Brummel said, smiling.

"I must have had a peculiar expression on my face," I said. "I mean, what were the odds of someone with that name living here? But of course now I had to go through with my little fiction. I watched Hans dialing you up, and I tried to think of what I would say. When he got you on the line, he said 'Ms. Brummel, there's a visitor here to see you. A Mister _____?' Here he gave me a look. 'Tell her it's Tom,' I said, 'from the old days.' If Hans thought this was strange, he didn't let on. 'It's a Tom from the old days,' he said. Then he handed me the phone. I should mention it was one of those old-fashioned phones we used to use. You know, attached to a cord. Anyway, I knew I'd painted myself in a corner, but I decided to play it out. The good news was that Hans couldn't hear what you were saying, so I could just pretend to set a lunch date and skip out of there. But when I said, 'Emma, this is Tom,' you replied 'Tom, it's wonderful to hear your voice!'"

"That I did," Emma Brummel said. "But before you go on, don't let the moisture in our glasses evaporate."

"How thoughtless of me," I said. I poured us each another round. "Funny how this bottle never seems to go empty. Have you noticed that, too?"

"I have not," Emma Brummel said. "Now do continue."

"Well, the rest of it I think you know," I said. "You pretended to recognize me, or maybe you thought I was some other Tom you already knew. You invited me to your apartment for a drink. And with Hans breathing down my neck, I decided to play along. So here we are."

"I don't remember any of that, though I'm sure it's how you say it is," Emma Brummel said.

"Of course," I said. "Funny how memories work."

"Indeed," Emma Brummel said.

There was a sharp knock at the door. Before either of us could respond, we heard the rattle of a key in the latch. The door swung open abruptly. There stood Hans in his blue concierge outfit, to which military medals were now affixed. He'd grown a salt and pepper beard since I'd seen him last.

"I'm afraid this conversation must be brought to a close," Hans said. With three quick strides, he crossed the room to where we sat. He seized Emma Brummel by the left arm. 'Brace yourself,' he said, and began to twist. Before I could react, her arm came off in one easy motion. Hans dropped it into an empty trunk by the foot of the bed—neither of which I'd noticed until this very moment.

"Please save the drinking arm for last," Emma Brummel said. She did not appear to be in pain.

"Very well, Ma'am," Hans said. He bent over and went to work on her right leg. Emma Brummel continued to sip from her glass.

"Well, look at the time," I said, rising to my feet. "I should probably be going."

There was a thud as Hans tossed the leg into the trunk.

"No need to rush on my account," Emma Brummel said. "Do be so kind as to pour one last splash."

Hans was by this time working on the left leg. I reached around him and refilled her glass.

"Bottoms up!" Emma Brummel said cheerfully.

"In due time," Hans said. The leg gave way with a snap.

"Well, it's been wonderful getting reacquainted," I said. I found myself backing toward the door.

"Do give some thought to what we talked about," Emma Brummel said. She gulped down the contents of her glass just as Hans seized hold of her head.

"Sir, you're welcome to stay if you wish," Hans said. He nodded toward the trunk. "There's plenty of room for you."

"Thank you. Perhaps another time," I said—and then I was out the door. I felt my heart lunging against my sternum. What had I just seen? I wandered the labyrinthine, gas-lit hallway, trying to remember how I got from the lobby to Emma Brummel's apartment. From time to time, I imagined I heard Hans's footsteps behind me, and I hastened my pace. After what might have been minutes, I saw a door with an Exit sign above it. Breathing a sigh of relief—and without a second thought--I pushed it open.

I found myself on a darkened street. Falcon Heights dissolved behind me. I tried to get my bearings, but no landmarks looked familiar. I looked one way and then the other. For as far as I could see, the street was bordered by stone wells that gleamed faintly in the light of a half moon. As my eyes adjusted, I detected shadowy forms moving about the wells. Then I recognized that they were children, silently raising and lowering wooden buckets.

At that moment, a figure detached itself from the shadows and approached me. I watched as it drew nearer and felt a tremor of uneasiness. It was no child but a cloaked stranger, just my height. The stranger stopped in front of me. For a moment, we regarded each other, though I could not see his face in the dim light. Then a voice slithered out from the darkness of his cowl. "Do you have any hand mirrors for sale?"

The question was so strange that a nervous spasm of laughter escaped my lips. "What? I beg your pardon? Who, exactly, do you think I am?" I asked. "Why would I have hand mirrors for sale?"

But then, much to my surprise, I found that I did.

Clairvoyant

First I was a candle whispering "fire," then a blur in need of naming.
Phrases dangled out of reach, so I became a small, still voice
channeled by famed medium Madam Lipinski. I could have been
the ghost behind your left shoulder or the ghost in front of you, saying
"Remember that trick I did with quantum particles when you were a kid?
It made you what you are today!" But before I could take credit,
I became a week of non-committal weather, followed by snow.
Next, a preacher lost his place, and so I daydreamed behind the wheel,
thinking "Some creatures dwell so deep in the sea that they make
their own light--the way I do behind closed eyes in dreams I won't remember. "
Nevertheless, I absorbed your puddle of tears using birdseed
I purchased from an old necromancer on Franklin Street. She told me
that the dead have no more idea of what the future holds than we do.
She also told me there are pages written that go unread—and that's
what I was next, an unread page, and that's what I remained for a long,
long time, until you dog-eared me, and then I was a night of crickets singing,
and then, just for a moment, I was you, turning the page—
and then I was something burning.

Adoration of the Magi's Guild

We are arranging to have your lucid sex dreams narrated by a medieval theologian.

A creel-full of baby teeth awaits your predilection in the gazebo.

Our engineers have designed special cantilevers known to induce spinal rapture; they've left a prototype in your tea room.

Generations of highly educated monks are devoting their lives to the purification of your orange chakra.

Your new contact lenses, made from the tears of unrequited lovers, will give you 20-20 vision in what you imagine is the dark.

Space-age fabrics with special wicking properties and trap doors are being assembled for your wardrobe by our top breeders.

Kitchen appliances for which no food has been invented, but which are said to have certain surgical applications and aphrodisiac qualities, are being delivered to your primary residence in unmarked ice cream trucks.

The sensation of a thousand moth wings has been captured in an aerosol spray, now approved for human subjects—and you, specifically.

We've printed glossy brochures guaranteed to attract more visitors to your Peccadillo Park.

Our scribes are rewriting all the epics per your instructions.

Guides raised as celibates are preparing a tour of your new belvedere on the Northern Coast. Those of us who imagine different lives for ourselves take solace in the sound of their jingling keys, one of which unlocks the secret chamber where a metal gurney awaits your anesthetization.

Vacation in the Catacombs

Years from which the days have been hollowed out.

Walls without function.

All the weather removed.

No need to buy a postcard. No need to fight for a window seat.

There may be some contention over verb tenses, or a minor skirmish over "Memory vs. memories."

"It's impossible to have a single memory," someone says, "without other memories attaching themselves. To remember the girl in the green bikini is also to remember her hair, her indifference, the beach where you saw her, what your friend said, what became of that friendship, and so on."

"Every memory sprouts from a wound," someone else says.

"Memories are what stitch our wounds together," says a third—was it you? Your voice sounds different in the dark, like God at a distance, or a real bell that is always about to ring.

The Usual

I forgot my name.

Then I remembered it again.

Then I forgot it.

This went on for some time.

During a lucid period, I decided to take my dog for a walk. Don't go too far, I reminded myself. Otherwise you might get lost. But of course, I forgot all about that. We walked and walked. After a time, we found ourselves in a strange part of the city. Tall, glassy office buildings surrounded us. I was hungry, but this looked like the wrong part of town to get a sandwich. I saw a doorman standing in front of the tallest building. "Excuse me," I said. "Could you direct me to a good deli?"

"Good afternoon, Mr. Belington," the doorman said. "Hungry, are we? Why don't you wait in your office and let us send someone out for you? Will it be the usual?"

"The usual?"

The doorman took out his phone. "Alice, could you send one of the interns to Moser's Deli? Mr. Belington will have the usual. And make it fast." He looked at me and smiled. "Anything else I can do for you. Sir?" He held the door open.

"No, that's fine," I said. Then I realized I didn't remember where my office was. I said, "Perhaps you could have someone assist me to my office. I seem to have misplaced my keys."

"Ask Charlene," the doorman said. "I'm sure she can help you."

"And where might I find her?" I asked.

The doorman's expression changed. "Is this some kind of test? Are you testing me?"

"No," I said. "I was simply asking—"

"What do you take me for?" the doorman snapped. "Some kind of fool? Someone who will swallow anything you care to dish out? It's bad enough that you steal her from me, but now you want to rub my nose in it—is that it? I love Charlene the way a river loves the sea. Someone like you will never know that kind of love. Never! You may be on top now, but my time will come. I used to run this business, and I swear someday I will run it again, and then maybe you can learn what it's like to wear this monkey suit and be compelled to behave in the most obsequious manner toward those you despise." He looked at my dog. "And you," he said. "You betrayed me, too."

"Now see here!" I said. "In the first place, my intention was not to hurt your feelings. And in the second place, I will not abide your speaking to me in this fashion. It's most inappropriate."

The doorman's face reddened. "What are you going to do?" he said. "Fire me?"

"I shouldn't like to do it, but I would if pressed," I said. "Your behavior is simply out of bounds."

The doorman shook his head sadly. "Unbelievable. Your own brother," he said. "Who'd have thought it would come to this?"

"What?"

"You would fire your own brother! Now I've heard everything! First, you steal his job. Then you steal his wife. Then you steal his dog. And after all that, once he's thoroughly humiliated, you fire him—put him out on the street like a pauper and force him to live under a bridge somewhere, begging for sustenance from total strangers. You would do that?"

"You're my brother?" I asked.

"You ask me that question! Mother and Father must be rolling in their graves," he said. "What would they say if they were alive—to hear you deny your older brother, your own flesh and blood, who watched over you and taught you how to hit a ball and helped pay for your education when Father died, who brought you into the family business and made you best man at his wedding! Have you not a single shred of compassion?"

"Alright, alright," I said. "I'm sorry. Just please don't raise your voice. I've been suffering from headaches lately. Bad headaches, if you must know. I'm really not myself. Forgive me if I seem out of sorts."

"It's a brother's duty to forgive," he said. "Remember that."

"I will," I said. Anxious to escape this unpleasantness, I ducked inside the door and found myself in an enormous lobby with polished granite flooring, leather furniture, and exotic potted plants. A backlit Belington Enterprises icon hung on the far wall, above the receptionist's desk. The receptionist herself caught my eye and held it. She was a stunning woman with auburn hair and full lips. She wore a low cut green dress. Her nametag said "Charlene." When she saw me approaching, she smiled. "Darling," she said, "you were gone a long time." She leaned over the desk and puckered her lips.

I gave her a quick peck. "Walking the dog," I said.

"And how is my little poochikins" she said. The dog wagged its tail enthusiastically.

"We got lost," I said. "He guided me here."

"He?"

"I mean she," I said. "Listen, could you come with me to my office? I seem to have lost my key."

"Why certainly," Charlene said demurely. She ran a finger along my solar plexus. "Maybe I can help you find that key."

"That would be helpful," I said.

We approached the elevator. "Listen, there's something I need to ask you," I said.

"What's that?"

The elevator door opened. We stepped inside. Charlene reached across me and pushed the button for the 60th floor, which was also the top floor. "It's about my brother," I said.

"Who?"

There was a ting! As the elevator door slid shut.

"My brother," I said. "You know, outside."

"I don't know what you're talking about," Charlene said. She started to undo my top button. The elevator began to rise.

"The doorman!" I said. "My older brother! The one who used to run this place."

"We don't have a doorman," Charlene said, going to work on the next button, and then the next.

"But I just talked to him! He said you were married to him and that I stole you away!"

"Don't be a silly goose," Charlene said. She slid a hand inside my shirt and began to trace light circles on my chest. The elevator went faster. "There never was a doorman," she said.

I decided not to press it. Instead, I gave in to the moment. Charlene and I kissed, long and deeply. I grabbed her ass, and comets fell about us, leaving long trails of light.

There was another ting! I looked up. Forty-fourth floor. Someone was getting on board. Charlene and I quickly disentangled ourselves as the doors slid open. There stood a young man who looked barely old enough to drink, wearing a white shirt, open at the collar, and dark slacks with a perfect crease. When he saw me, his green eyes flashed. "Ah, Mr. Belington," he said, smiling. "I was just on my way up to see you!" He held up a brown paper bag.

"What's that?" I said.

"It's for you," he said. "Your order."

I took the bag.

Still a little confused, I said "What order is that?"

"You know." He gave me what seemed a too-familiar wink. "The usual," he said, and the elevator doors slid shut.

Twilight in an Imaginary Antipodes

Certainly you were coming home later than usual—
that's what I thought, waiting on the front porch swing,
your diary open on my lap. In fact, you had already
returned unnoticed and were sleeping soundly upstairs,
the streetlight outside your window, a beacon for mayflies,
covering you in a silver blanket.
Well, what *isn't* a reiteration of the moon?
That kind of light is always scrubbing something clean,
scouring words from our own pages and replacing them
with a phosphorous snowfall.
What could I write that could leave a footprint?
What could I write that you might trace?
I was ready to confront you with these questions,
ready to confront you with your own words,
when I heard boot steps on the porch. I looked up.
Enter the antagonist, Tantalus Tombstone.
He has a face like something seen from the corner of your
eye. When he draws near, I can hear his teeth grinding.
His clothes smell of canal water and regret.
What moments ago seemed a suburban tableau
festooned with ribbons of nostalgia now seems
something else altogether. "You're here to ruin this poem,
aren't you?" I ask. He extends a bony finger, like a
ghost out of Dickens, and touches your diary.
In a blink, the words melt and run off the page.
They form a dark puddle at my feet. "Now you've done it!
I was reading that!" I tell him. "In fact, I was going to
end this poem by quoting from it."
"I have a better ending," he replies.
He reaches out and touches my forehead.

Second Session

Holding a Séance by Myself

A ghost that won't explain itself is best.

Why is it drawn to doilies? Can it communicate only by sneezing?
Where did it hide my pince-nez?

A ghost understands that endings are the price we pay for narrative.

This is why most ghosts are nothing but repetition—which is their charm.

Of course, I have my preferences. I have learned to summon certain
types of ghosts.

The dead son who appears as a reflection in his father's monocle is far too
personal.

The ghost of a tree that superimposes itself over another tree is more to
my liking.

There is a ghost for everything we forget, including dreams.

There is a ghost for everything we remember too much.

I keep your ghost in the closet to remind me of when I was alive. It's easier
than calling you on the phone.

There are ghosts who do nothing but climb into your words. It's surprising the
way they appear out of nowhere, ready to speak for you.

But that's the price of being a medium.

Even now, I can't tell if it's them or me writing this.

Sidewinder

Will there be a refrain? I asked. You know, something
to help me get a toehold, or even a leg up? Nope.
Snake-bosomed, harpsicords for knees, shy as a male mantis.
Who's taking whom to the ritual harvest dance?
I see a big empty space where a kiss should be.
If a tree doesn't fall far from the apple, does it make a sound?
Count the rings. Only the burnt tongue speaks to God.
The burnt hand may tap Him on the shoulder, meekly.
Apparently He likes His steaks well done.
Accordion spleen. Geiger-counter heart. Hourglass liver.
Whether you think of salmon as pink or silver says a lot about you.
I'd trade these words for a chance at something.
We set so many barriers for ourselves.
She was naked and covered in salamanders.
The salamanders, of course, were sacred and not to be touched.
I could use that refrain right about now.
Sharp edges aren't meant to be caressed. Yet I go on.
There's a kind of contentment in this wallpaper. The Sunday light
through sliding glass patio doors belongs to someone else now
—all but this ladle-full. Captain Bly, shall I release the dragon?
The roller coaster paused at the apex, just long enough
for us to see there were no more tracks.
Combination locks for elbows. Xylophone teeth. Wishes for fingers.
They're playing our song. The downward plunge commences.

Taking the High Road by Another Route

Whether time inheres in a photograph,
the paper remains acidic, it browns, it yellows,
and the years stand on street corners like schoolboys, smoking,
until they catch themselves reminiscing about
the last cigarette—a misplaced nostalgia--and no one
at the covered dish supper would touch Mrs. Baumgartner's
corn casserole in its floral-patterned bowl
because it was ahead of its time. I took the cue
and wouldn't touch it either, and then suddenly I remembered
that the way you scratched your dog's belly was deemed 74%
obscene by The Ladies' Consistory; the dog knew it, too, believe me;
I can't remember its name, some kind of hound, pink tongue lolling;
it was always hot when I drove by your house,
big-bully sun, hiss of cicadas, lawn mowers struggling
on your yard's steep slope; I wouldn't try that; I wouldn't;
we didn't call it "summer" then; in those days
seasons' names were numerical,
proper nouns were still being invented,
I couldn't name that spot you touched, on the dog I mean,
and I wouldn't now; too much time has been
gambled away, as we like to say never,
and in your honor I've memorized all the coordinating
conjunctions, or maybe I haven't, for what
reason would I?—so I could remind myself
of what I wouldn't say? --but that's not funny,
nor is it apropos, yet like a stubborn tide it washes
over everything. I wouldn't swim in it.
I wouldn't time the silence between foghorn blasts.
I wouldn't trust the lifeguard—how can he hear a
panicked cry over that song on his transistor radio?
Back then, we called it Song 152;
everyone imagined space flight, but no one would try it;
loneliness was made of tinsel,
the government ruled by telepathy,
all cars were blue,

sinkholes appeared on a regular basis,
most of us lived on a cul de sac—
but you lived on a road that overlooked the cul de sac,
and that has made all the difference.
Besides, in those days stars shone with subtler kinds of light,
salt tasted like consternation,
and we wouldn't even try to imagine what lurked in that casserole.
All the slithery things were strictly in my head.

Spring Break

"Excuse me, is this the road to the necropolis?"

Hard to believe just hours ago we were sipping Cuba libres on the patio, while someone played a celesta in the distance—which was where we preferred it, frankly.

You observed how laky the sky looked, as the broken wind swept over us in intermittent gusts from the sea, and I felt more nescient than ever in my pastel beachwear.

And now—was this really a journey to the underworld? I wish I could say it was unexpected, but these old parables never are! Even the way the gnarled trees copped a feel as we passed—it was the same tired theatricalism, leading inevitably to bleeding and self-discovery.

Or was it avoidable this time? Can these pilgrims be rerouted, say, to an air conditioned strip mall, or at least someplace where the lottery tickets are less consequential?

Maybe we could watch reruns of your last metempsychosis over a nice glass of rye? Or gird our loins by the fire? We could invent a new adverb or two and cauterize this allegory until it turns postmodern and oxymoronic.

Although I must say this dark wood really brings out the ennui in your eyes. So there's that.

Lapis Lazuli

We were lost. The horses were dead.

In the light of our desert campfire, you studied a map that wouldn't stop coughing.

You said, "There are no night birds in this region," which seemed to be true. No night birds. I hadn't noticed before you said it.

I'd been dragging my saddle, still wet with blood, behind me for what seemed like days. It was the saddle Pappy gave me, the one with his initials monogrammed on the cantle, but it had grown heavy.

"Ahead this way lies a land of many gaps," you said. "Perhaps there I will find some lapis lazuli."

"You mean 'we,'" I said.

We were lost. The horses were dead.

The wind blew down from the mountain. The canyon walls shimmered as if they were still underwater, as if The Great Sea still covered us.

"Beyond the land of many gaps lies a village where we can fill our canteens," you said, "but the wells are guarded by spirits. As you lower your bucket into the well, they will try to guess your name. If they succeed before you can draw the water and drink it, you become one of them."

"I like those odds," I said. "Thaddeus Demetrius Thornwhistle III won't be the first name they conjure."

"The spirits don't guess your birth name," you said. "They guess your *true* name—the one your mother never told you, the one that defines you, the one that, when you utter it, conjures you into being."

"Don't reckon I know that one, myself," I said.

"You'll know if they guess it," you said. "But the lapis lazuli is worth the risk. For the lapis lazuli, all suffering is redeemed. When I gaze into the lapis lazuli—"

"When *we* gaze," I said.

You fell silent. I began to wonder what sort of guide you were. You seemed to know many things about the way ahead, but little about where we were now.

Who cared about night birds? Land of many gaps? What kind of gaps?

We were lost. The horses were dead. The canyon walls shimmered.

The map coughed and coughed, covering itself with phlegm.

Was your compass myopic? Could we follow the North Star?

"Listen!" you said, raising a finger in the air, though I hadn't been talking, except in my head. I listened. Just past the fire-light's perimeter, something was circling, making whimpering noises in the dark. I listened closer and realized there were more than one, whatever it was. Coyotes? Had the scent of blood drawn them in?

I would have to leave Pappy's saddle behind. My sole inheritance.

"What should we do?" I said.

You took out a small mirror and examined your reflection, brushing back a stray wisp of hair. "How much lapis lazuli can one man carry across the desert?" you said, more to the mirror than to me.

"You mean two men!" I shouted. "Besides, what does it matter? We're lost. I'm beginning to think we'll never find lapis lazuli. I'm beginning to think you have no idea where we are or where we have to go. You're the guide! Do you even know the way?"

You turned and held the mirror to my face. "Do you even know what a way is?" you said.

We were lost. The horses were dead. The North Star shimmered as if it couldn't stay lit. The canyon walls, too—everything shimmered, as if The Great Sea still covered us.

Reflections on My Long, Torrid Summer

In May, you left me, the way Rimbaud left literature.

In June, I became a quantum real estate agent. My slogan was "Location, velocity, location."

A box of nothing was stirred by the eye that opened it.

Several hearts took up shadow boxing.

I experienced audio hallucinations: one morning I woke, but the song I'd been dreaming about kept playing. It was the most beautiful song I'd ever heard, and it seemed so real that I left my apartment and went out in search of its source. But it was me—or rather, I was an antenna, and the source was unknown.

You moved to a far-off city and became an investment counselor, mostly in order to establish dramatic irony, but also to irritate me. My friends tried to console me, saying you were lost at sea or suffering from syphilitic paralysis, but I didn't believe them.

A shortage of onomatopoeia made headlines.

An invasive species of rhetorical parasite was observed in town halls and state houses.

Some songbirds began to sing in three-quarter time.

Graffiti was discovered on Mars. Translators remained baffled.

In July, I read Nietzsche's *Will To Power*, using your picture as a bookmark.

I moonlighted as a symphony chef, a polisher of bannisters, a fletcher of arrows that wouldn't shoot straight, and a liturgist.

A box of horizons was spilled by a woman no one recognized.

I saw a white butterfly die in mid-air.

I heard rumors you'd become a water dowser and had written a treatise on ideomotor phenomena. Were my feelings returning?

I tried to contact you on a Ouija board, but the only spirit I could reach was someone named Elisa. We promised to marry this fall, once my political career gets underway.

In August, I became aware of something crawling underneath my words, which had begun to detach themselves from their meanings—though what they were attaching to, instead, I couldn't say.

I saw your face in a photo of Antarctic explorers.

Another box arrived, but no one opened it.

I scanned the Help Wanted ads and saw "Sextant Needed" printed over and over. This explained the absence of bells. It was one of the summer's few satisfactory explanations for anything.

Some translators decided that the Martian graffiti was a logographic language. Others observed that the symbols slanted to the left, which indicated a lack of emotion on the part of the writer. But what did they know?

All searched in vain for any reference to life on earth.

Where Are They Now?

One became caught on the fly-wheel of a notion;
another clung to the hem of disbelief.
A third wandered in the Valley of Exegetes,
clutching Beauty's discarded raiment in his arms, and weeping;
a fourth watched crocuses bloom from his stigmata;
a fifth chewed through allegorical legs ensnared
in allegorical traps; a sixth built a vaudeville stage in his brain,
but the only entertainment he could find was a travelling troupe
of medieval actors performing morality plays; a seventh got lost
in the mirror maze, yet never saw his reflection;
an eighth got with child a mandrake root, then agonized
over what to name it and whether it would be
better off in private school; a ninth picked pockets
in other peoples' dreams; a tenth claimed to be a whistle-blower
in a corrupt financial institution—except the whistle
was a dog-whistle, and those he alerted were the
perpetrators of crimes against the poor;
an eleventh attached handles to everything; a twelfth said
"Terrible is the arc of our lives, and more terrible still
the oblique shadows we cast upon each other;
a thirteenth stammered through the benediction
and never quite made it to the end.

It's Time

It's time to tether-ball that notion,
to give it a few good whacks; time to
vacate the arboretum, to unfurl
the scroll of incantations and to summon
more than the usual moths, the usual
sparrows; time to stop pretending angels
are personal; time to fully grasp what it
means to be a martyr without a cause;
it's time to anachronize your watches,
time to slip into something less comfortable,
to riddle the sphinx for a change; time
to see who's peeping through the keyhole,
to knock down balustrades, to
look up "crepuscular" and use it in a
grocery list, to harrow an icon—any icon,
but preferably a religious one;
time to throw pepper over your right shoulder;
time to forget that "egg-and-gyroscope" business;
time to tune a forklift, to launch a missile
of laughing gas, to call the Lithuanians and
offer forgiveness; time to put the kibosh on
all that sighing and pretending to have fooled
the Inspector; time to stop charging us
to watch you sleep; time to switch to low-salt,
secular relics, to become neutron-free, to join a
lens-grinder's guild; time to dance with the illusion
that brought you, to perforate that mirage, even
though it made your daddy rich; time to drive the car;
time to feed the bears, to buy a subway map,
to eat of the air, promise-crammed; time to
wait for the next Big Subject with a butterfly net
—which, face it, is all you've got, though its
webbing is weak and its holes the wrong size;
time to wax your paradigms; time to recycle
the *cantus firmus*, to fire on all cylinders;
time to stop, just stop, please stop.

Shoelaces

In your brain, words swim in custard,
a man sits by a window thinking,
"'Space' and 'time' are middle terms between
my perceptions and myself." Don't bother him.
Just leave him be. Around the corner
sits a vat of floating eggs; over here, one corridor leads
to the cathedral, another to the arena;
here, a Bach fugue and a Robert Johnson song play simultaneously;
crowds gather at the launch pad; someone's burning
post cards in the high school parking lot; a man
recites a soliloquy before imagined ancestors—ignore him.
avoid landscapes where you might be "overheard."
Here's where the mannequins are constructed; here's the
pratfall station; here's a meaningless box of shoelaces.
That sound you hear may be some of these words drowning;
that smell may be eucalyptus. Here's the woman
who threatened to eat your dog; here's the woman
who poured wine by the sea; here's the woman
who called you a liar, who said "There never
was a man. There never was a window."

Recital

Mr. Indecision sets his crutches down and takes a seat before the piano. "Here's a little atonal piece by tennis-pro-turned-composer Guy Monteblanc," he says. "It's called *Marimba Wood*, or something like that." Then, fingers poised above the keys, he begins to weep. The weeping begins as a gentle shower but quickly evolves into a violent storm. His shoulders convulse. Blue tears stream from his eyes. Enormous, racking sobs resonate through the music hall.

"What's wrong with him?" I ask.

"He has to do this for seven minutes and forty-one seconds," says Mr. I-Read-The-Program.

"So it's part of the piece? Interesting! Would you say it's from Monteblanc's expressionist period?" I ask.

"Dadaist," says Mrs. Professor. "The weeping is ironic. There is no Guy Monteblanc. The spoken introduction is part of the composition. The real author is Balaz Lakatos, a Hungarian unicyclist-turned-poet. The real name of the piece is "Fingers Magee." Mr. Indecision is performing it beautifully!"

"But if he's performing the piece as written, then why is his name Mr. Indecision? Is that ironic, too?"

"Hey, Mr. Why-Don't-You-Shut-Up, give it a rest. It's just a name," says Mr. Last Word.

Soviet Love Sonnet in Translation

Astonished by her onyx façade, her hooks;
Bedizened by her dime store glances;
Unappareled by the stolen turnips of her bosom;
her courtesan knees, her ontological instep;
Benighted by her unswerving migrations
and the imbroglio of her eyelashes,
which curve into future Wednesdays like love's
rented tuxedos awaiting the dry cleaner;
I, a lowly peddler, a hangnail, an itch unworthy of scratching,
swim in the borscht of her indifference, cold and pink,
the bassoon of desire laving my one good ear.
Nadia, Nadia, do you not care one soft sign for me?
I genuflect within the bounds of my restraining order,
hoping you might mitigate my presbyopic amours.

Recalcitrant Muse, Pathetically Invoked

"What we must remember," the TV man said, "is that
birds don't think of their songs as songs." But is it true?
Can the little icepick chirp of a cardinal be the product of
an aesthetic system? On this matter, Daughter of Memory,
you are strangely silent. Come to think of it, you haven't
said much for weeks, sitting there with your non-symbolic
vacuum cleaner attachment. Must I snap you out of another funk?
Third time this summer! Maybe you're listening to the wrong music,
the wrong weatherman, the wrong panegyrics. Remember that
time you set my brain on the windowsill, like a pie cooling,
and took me to the beach? "Reason always slows you down,"
you said, then pointed to a hand-operated potato masher half-
buried in the sand. I must have stared for hours. Why can't we have
those days back? Remember how we strained each other's feelings
through a sieve? I do, though of what the sieve consisted I can't recall.
Remember the appliances that made housework a breeze?
Convection ovens were your favorite. I didn't understand,
as my education was lacking. "Convection always takes place
through advection, diffusion, or both," you always said to me,
so patiently you should have been a saint—maybe the one with the arrows.
Or better yet, Saint Francis of Assisi. Then you could have weighed in
on this birdsong business. You still could! Please come to!
Tell me that any intentional cry can be a song. Take me
to your favorite grove and teach me about Brownian motion.
I'll bring the devilled eggs. You can leave my brain anyplace you like.

A Few Words Thrown Short of Their Target

On a moon-rinsed beach littered with runes, I'm picking up bad radio signals in my teeth —No! I am tired of "prescient dawns" and confabulatory prosthetics and those tiny red-headed birds you always claimed to see when my back was turned—No! This frost-bitten right shoe portends a diagnosis of "creeping metonymy" for your senior years, along with buttered peas and palm fronds and an attendant who speaks in iambic tetrameter—No! A swarm of nuthatches circle an imaginary birdhouse in Tennessee—No! A deaf-mute masseuse who works in the dark becomes your secret confidante—No! The sound of your dog lapping water from a bowl induces dropsy—No! At the Conference of Saints, you overhear a conversation about the divinity of the metrical system and The Magic Cantilevers of Zachariah—No! Ich habe einer Dorn in meiner Seele— Nein! The only sign of life was the Luna moth flitting behind her eyes— No! The Tall Ones are infiltrating our prayers—No! Bird-Headed Woman, smelling of burnt wool, why do you bring me faulty memories garnished with the entrails of mice? Go back to your lighthouse—No! From childhood on, Mercedes suffered from recurring stigmata that smelled like buttered popcorn—No! In The Metaphysician's Bowling Alley, I couldn't find shoes my size—No! This gold-plated ecclesiastical shoehorn is strictly decorative— No! Today I ate applesauce with a clear plastic fork, which worked better than expected and so filled my heart with renewed hope for myself and humankind—No! I'm in The Forest of Shaken Trees where there is no wind, recalling lives that cannot be mine, listening to the pedal-tone of a God I don't believe in reminding me how we've forsaken ourselves again and again--

Zeitgeist

I was searching in the closet for my missing Zeitgeist.

I couldn't find it, but I did come upon your diary, with its faux leather binding and cheap padlock, lying on the shelf beneath father's gray fedora (may he rest in peace). I remembered how, every night before coming to bed, you'd retreat to the study and scratch a few lines. Why hadn't you taken it with you when you left? Was it because our days together meant so little? What had you written about me? I decided to pursue these questions later, after I'd found my Zeitgeist.

The next place I looked was under the bed. There was nothing there—just a few dust balls, your sock, and a boogie man, curled up in the fetal position, muttering softly in his sleep. His skin was gray and wrinkled, like one of those Chinese dogs, but he looked so comfortable I decided not to wake him.

I opened the refrigerator and pulled out the vegetable tray. Onion skins— nothing more.

Then I remembered the tool shed. When was the last time I'd looked in there? It would be a perfect hiding place. No one would expect me to set foot in it. I wasn't what they call a "handy man"—as you were always quick to point out. Maybe you wrote an entry or two on that subject!

I went out back. Night had draped itself over the town. Dew clung to the uncut grass. The tool shed stood on my yard's far edge. Jewel weed and creeping vines had grown around it, and the bird bath was filled with soggy brown leaves. A rusty push mower leaned against the door. I set it aside and pushed the door open, the creaking hinges a perfect counterpoint to the cicada's buzz. Then I heard a gurgling noise, and, instead of being greeted by darkness as expected, I observed a greenish, phosphorescent light flickering on the ceiling and walls. Looking down, I was shocked to see that the wooden floor had disappeared into a large sinkhole or crater in which a glowing liquid bubbled up. All my tools were gone, having apparently been swallowed up in this newly formed cauldron. I leaned over and peered into it. Perhaps this was one of those healing springs I'd always heard about, the kind that cured arthritis and respiratory ailments. I breathed deeply as the warm mist reached my face. Almost instantly, a wave of dizziness passed over me. When I closed my eyes, colored spots swirled against my eyelids. My knees buckled, and I tipped forward. Before I knew it, I was swimming in the warm brine. My feet couldn't touch bottom. I kicked frantically, trying not to breathe the fumes, afraid I'd black out. My heart clenched like a fist. My lungs turned to pumice. Somehow I managed to pull myself out of the hole, and I lay on my back, gasping.

I felt as though some sort of current was passing through me, lighting circuits I'd never known were there. My skin was humming. Something seemed to be flitting behind my eyes. I needed to get further from the crater, so I crawled across the yard to the house. Only there did it occur to me to stand. I faltered on my first attempt, but then I grasped hold of the back porch railing and managed to pull myself up. I took a few deep breaths.

My whole body tingled. My flesh seemed to be undergoing some sort of transformation, though from what to what I could not say. I became acutely aware of my eyes and the fact that everything I'd ever seen in my life was just a reflection in a bubble, a pattern of light interference, a veil. Even the meteors streaking the sky seemed a shorthand version of something else. I could almost hear them, and the hearing and seeing were interwoven in a way for which I had no words. At least not yet.

I went back into the house. I was about to go upstairs when I noticed light under the study door. I pressed my ear against it. Someone was in there—I could feel it. I reached for the knob. It felt electric in my hand, its atoms jangling against mine, but I managed to give it a twist. The door swung open.

My Zeitgeist sat in the leather arm chair, wearing a black smoking jacket. The desk lamp reflected off his monocle. Your diary lay open on his lap. "If it's any consolation," he said, "this isn't very interesting. Pretty pedestrian, in fact. What I had for dinner, and that kind of thing."

"Am I mentioned?" I asked.

My Zeitgeist flipped through the pages. "Here and there," he said. "Nothing particularly revelatory. I wouldn't worry about it. You have bigger concerns now."

"What do you mean?"

My Zeitgeist closed the diary. "I see you've been swimming," he said. "Feeling okay?"

Even as he said it, the humming in my skin grew louder, or, more accurately, it began to diffuse through me--or I through it. I felt as though I was dissolving into white noise. "What's happening to me?"

"I don't know. It's a new age," my Zeitgeist said.

I was about to ask what he meant when I noticed steam coming up through the floorboards. The house began to tremble. I could hear the boogie man howling upstairs. "What's up with him?" I asked, but my Zeitgeist was no longer there, and then neither was I.

Third Session

Critique

In a rare and ancient book on Ornithology I read that the female goldfinch trails her brilliantly colored mate like a sad shadow, that blue jays have tin ears, and that crows with highly developed aesthetic sensibilities tend to be overly critical, which facts seemed unscientific to me until a crow appeared at my study room window and, uninvited, began to speak, saying "Please remember, human, that what you call our 'songs' cannot be replicated with your phonetics, that your 'caws,' 'tweets,' 'twitters,' and 'chirps' are pale equivalents, and that all around you we communicate in a language you can neither reproduce nor understand, which perhaps is why you impose upon it the armature of fear and lust that drives your own tongues so incessantly—your sailor's curses and your overwrought love songs, and all of your other talking monkey abstractions."

"That may be true, crow," I said, "but you forget that we humans express ourselves using complex syntactical systems and verbal nuances that your feathered friends can never hope to master—and what's more, we have writing!"

"Ah, that verbal excrescence you call 'writing,'" the crow said mockingly, "is proof to us of your language's fallibility and shortcomings, for if you could express yourself fully and truthfully in the moment, you would have no need to ascribe names to all things, thereby isolating yourselves from them at every turn, while deluding yourselves with the illusion of mastery over them—and furthermore, none of our trees would have to sacrifice their lives to preserve your cherished ambiguities and faulty memories and thwarted desires"—and with that, he flew away to a stand of tall pines where, for the rest of the day, I heard him and his companions cackling (if that's the word) as I struggled to write this down.

Age of Enlightenment

I put that book on aesthetics through the wood chipper.
The Sirens could not rival the sound it made.
Then I gathered the sawdust and mixed it with birdseed.
You were working on your new historical novel
and didn't notice when the birds began to grow more colorful,
their flight more graceful, their songs more complex. Sometimes
a group of them would sing in harmony, right by your window.
But you were engrossed in your character's wardrobe.
Mattie was a poor seamstress in 19th century London—
a comely lass who'd caught the roving eye of Sir Gilbert.
Upon the course of their interactions Mattie's fortunes
and reputation depended. Because clothing figured prominently
in the story, you'd researched cage crinoline, chemisettes, Berthas,
as well as frock coats, cravats and bowlers. You'd worked out in detail
the connections between fashion and social class, charting the
sartorial path along which Mattie's sewing would take her.

I swallowed a handful of the sawdust and seed. I stood in the yard,
arms akimbo, waiting for its effects. Soon I felt porous,
like I was made of light. I heard a sound like wind through a
crystal chandelier. Birds of gold, teal, and scarlet circled overhead,
then perched on my outstretched arms. I hoped you would see us,
but you didn't. You didn't even see that the house was ablaze,
though nothing was burning. As we watched you through the window,
hunched over your keyboard, we knew how your novel would end.

The Feral Man

The once famous feral child, now grown to adulthood, walks among us unobserved, shielded from ostracism by his suit and tie. Years ago, his picture adorned every newspaper, and some of us still remember the bared teeth, tangled hair, and, most of all, the eyes, which until his discovery had peered from caves and stalked prey in a forest glen. Today, you could pass him on the street and never know it, for in appearance he is quite ordinary, neat and clean-shaven, and he has adapted to the ways of his human tribe, blending almost seamlessly into society, so that only the most acute observer—or perhaps another feral child— could detect in his public behavior any sign of his non-human upbringing. He speaks fluently without accent and, like us, he has acquiesced to the need for money, earned through labor. He maintains a modest third floor apartment and works nine to five in an office downtown, where his unwitting colleagues think him a decent fellow and a reasonably diligent worker, though perhaps from time to time a little distant, a little detached. But is that so unusual? Who doesn't erect barriers against the prating foolishness of his companions when the situation warrants it? Who hasn't fashioned a protective shell in order to preserve one's soft, inner self from the whips and scorn of everyday human treachery?

Of course, the feral man's "self" differs qualitatively from that of his peers in subtle ways he does not fully understand. This may be so because his childhood memories remain shadowy, without a scaffolding of words to map them onto memory—and therefore they maintain a stronger hold on him than would ordinary, human memories, which tend to compartmentalize experience into "themes" and "concepts." His human nature, as it were, remains planted in the dark, loose soil of another nature entirely. Its roots still derive nourishment from that soil. But because those roots are buried and therefore invisible to him, he remains aware of his split condition without being able to express, in human terms, what half of it consists of. Furthermore, the boundaries between his native and adopted selves tend to blur, making it hard to determine, at any given moment, which one is driving his actions.

And so, when early in the morning before showering and shaving for work, he perches naked upon the windowsill, makes whimpering sounds, licks his lips, and shivers slightly as a young woman walks her Pomeranian past him on the sidewalk below, who's to say whether it is his animal or his human nature manifesting itself in its essential, undisguised form?

Not My House

The house I call "mine" in dreams
is not my house.

Attic rooms change size. Dusty trunks
and tailor's dummies vanish and reappear.

At the shadowy ends of hallways,
coffin-sized grandfather clocks tick and tock.

Water gurgles beneath the floorboards.

And in the basement—a cistern
I refuse to peer into!

No, this crawl space in the cerebellum
cannot be my house.

Or if it is my house, then whose dark portrait
hangs above the mantel?

If it is my house, then who shuttered
all the windows overlooking the sea?

If it is my house, then who is this child who follows me,
this child tugging at my sleeve and whispering over and over

"The dreamer's eye is a skeleton key"
till his words blaze like a comet through my waking hours?

Check, Please

Order up some homiletic soup. Three tureens.
Someone's stopping bullets in Texas, Lord;
someone's driving a Plymouth and working for Nabisco.
I ought to get more fiber. Problem is, Lord,
too many tunnels are collapsing. Wait for a
greener day, wait for gainsayers—that's popular
opinion, everyone has one, so said the melismatic
jeweler with six fingers, as his gypsy wife smiled demurely;
all of her fortune-telling is conjectural, Lord; I've been promised
so many things: cake, maypoles, a new inner ear,
a drink poured in Lichtenstein, a poet's ratchet,
inoculations against policy, a forehead gasket.
Times were simpler when all the canneries operated
at full capacity, Lord. We could count on massive
government overreach. I had something inside out
for a pet, but it wasn't leash-trained. You could hear
Russian voices on walkie-talkies during the full moon.
New moons, the batteries died. I looked for you, Lord,
but you wore an invisible hat. I worried that
you would leave me and move to Texas. Then you
left me and moved to Texas. Diners there served
prayers- on-a-stick. One preacher had a gray bird he liked to talk to.
All of the tunnels were named after religious martyrs.

Dark

It is darker in this corner of the poem.
I observe this darkness, and what I see
fills me with questions. Does darkness bind together
what the light holds separate? Or does it divide us
from everything? Are we more, or less, ourselves in the dark?
What would that mean? Is it true that sounds
become clearer in the dark? Or is there a kind
of darkness that smothers sound? Can it be so dark
that the darkness can no longer be seen? Can it be so dark
that all we see is the world we live in, and nothing more?

Walking the Manticore

"Is he friendly?" asked the woman with the toy poodle.

"Well—" I began.

"Madame, if I may," the manticore interjected, "your curly-haired companion has nothing to fear from me. I'm a mythological beast, my appetites strictly allegorical—my teeth, barbs, and scorpion tail merely some ancient Babylonian's fever dream."

"Do you hear that, Fifi? Say hello to the nice manticore," the woman said, slackening the leash. The poodle edged forward and sniffed the manticore's snout. The manticore stood stock still, expressionless. Then, emboldened, the poodle wandered toward its hind end, where it took further inventory, planting its nose at the base of the manticore's tail. Soon its own tail began to wag furiously, like a flag of surrender.

"He's very well trained," the woman remarked. "Has he been through obedience school?"

"You might say a few have been through him," I replied.

"What?"

Just then, the manticore began to hum softly, starting on a note unexpectedly high, given his fierce countenance, then sliding down a silvery scale into what might be considered a human range.

"Oh, my! What's he doing?" the woman asked. She stood, transfixed.

The melody unfurling from the manticore's throat was hauntingly beautiful— one I'd never heard before. But then, the manticore never repeated his tunes as far as I was aware. He was like a Siren with an unlimited repertoire, each performance unique—and uniquely effective. Just looking at the woman, whose eyes were already brimming with tears, I could see that, once again, the manticore had selected a melody custom-made for his listener, one that tapped into personal memories and emotions, giving them form without substance, making them irresistible. She began to tremble.

"He's singing for his supper," I said, but she was already gone.

The poodle looked baffled at first. Then it began to run in circles, whimpering. The manticore watched it dispassionately. "I suppose we'll have to find another park," it said, licking a stray drop of blood.

"I suppose we will," I replied.

After a minute, the poodle, realizing it was free, trotted toward the woods. At the boundary, it paused to lift its leg and regard us for a few seconds; then, as if suddenly recalling a prior engagement, it turned and slinked into the dark undergrowth, trailing its leash behind it.

Signs of the Times

The half-forgotten prophet has returned,
bearing a homewrecker's smile and a
chalice full of syzygy. I hope he doesn't leave a mess
for the cleaning lady. I hope he doesn't
fiddle with the stereo; I like my settings just so.
I wish he'd stop giving me these scrolls to read.
My preference is to gaze out the window.
These rainy June days bring many new forms of wildlife.
Right now I'm listening to a bird whose cry sounds
like a razor through vermillion. It's another sign
of the times, the prophet informs me. Have I noticed
they seem to be multiplying? Have I noticed
the surplus of shadows? Have I noticed things getting
blocked by other things? These days, everyone
is offering interpretations, but the problem is that
their interpretations lead to even newer signs of
newer times. I should spend more time undoing
the old signs, he suggests. Then he starts to paint
astrological symbols on the living room ceiling.
"An end to corners!" he shouts. "An end to fluorescence!"
His hair is wet, and he's wearing my bath towel.
"How do I know you're not a false prophet?" I ask him.
"You don't even have a beard." "Haven't you heard?" he says.
"The Age of Skepticism has ended. This is The Age of Accounts Vary."
 points to the window. Outside, in the gathering dark,
humming-bird-sized fireflies form new and ever-changing
glyphs of light as they chew up the geraniums.

Druthers

The package with my druthers arrived this morning. I knew it would be here—
I'd been following the tracking information since the day I ordered it. I even
called in sick to work so I could be here when it arrived. I stood on the front
porch and watched the delivery man carrying the package up my driveway.
"Thanks," I said as he handed it over. "Looks like it's gonna be a nice day."

"Hope so," the delivery man said. "They were calling for rain, but it's beautiful
now."

It's working already! I thought, bearing the package quickly into the house. I
set it on the kitchen table, then took a steak knife and slit through the packing
tape. I opened the lid, pulled out a wad of bubble wrap, and there it was! My
druthers. It was smaller than I'd expected, fitting easily in the palm of my hand.
Also, I'd imagined it would be more colorful—and shiny, with lots of moving
parts. Instead, it was gray, with one fold in the middle. Well, how was I to
know? I'd never had my own druthers before. Besides, it didn't matter what it
looked like, as long as it worked. But I'll confess, the thought that my druthers
might not be as dazzling or powerful as someone else's did nag at me a little.
After, all, I'd bought it on sale.

The sound of my phone chirping broke that train of thought. I glanced at the
screen. It was my boss. "Hello?" I said, trying to sound sick.

"George! How are you? When I heard you called in sick, I was beside myself
with worry."

"Really?" I said. I stared at my druthers.

"Of course," my boss said. "How are you feeling?"

"I'm a little under the weather," I said, adding a cough for emphasis. "Probably
one of those twenty-four-hour bugs."

"Do you need anything? Cough medicine? Chicken soup? I could bring some
soup over this afternoon," my boss said, sounding almost desperate to help.

"That won't be necessary," I said. "A little rest should do the trick. I imagine I'll be back in the office tomorrow."

"Well, when you get here, be sure to stop in and see me right away so we can talk about your promotion," he said. "It's about time we pay you what you're worth."

"Sounds good," I said. Was it my imagination, or could I feel my druthers tingling? Then I heard a blip. I looked down at my screen and saw another call was coming through—my daughter. "Listen, I have to take another call," I said.

"It's not Rob McIntyre from Techtron, is it?" my boss asked. "Because if it is, you can tell him we'll top any offer he makes you."

"It's not Rob McIntyre," I said. "It's my daughter. Gotta go."

I hung up on him. "Hi, honey," I said.

"Oh, Dad," my daughter exclaimed, her voice quivering. "I'm so, so sorry!"

"For what? What's wrong?" I asked.

"I'm so ashamed I can hardly talk about it," she said. She began to cry.

"Just tell me what's wrong. It can't be that bad," I said.

"Luke and I have been talking," she said, regaining her composure. "We realize now it was wrong to name Billy after Luke's dad. After all, Luke's got four brothers who could name their kids after him, whereas I'm your only daughter."

"Well, that's water under the bridge," I said, tossing and catching my druthers in my left hand. "Besides, you should name your son after whomever you like. He's your child."

"No!" my daughter said. "It was thoughtless of us. But we'd like to make amends. Luke and I talked it over just now, and we've decided to change his name to George William."

"Won't that be complicated?" I asked. "He's twelve years old. He may not want to change it."

"Oh, he's all for it. He thinks 'George' is much cooler than 'Billy.' He says he can hardly wait to be named after his favorite grandpa. He's been bragging about it to all his friends."

"That's nice," I said. "But just to be clear . . . you were still planning to keep William as his middle name?"

There was a moment of silence. "Well, of course we don't have to," she said. "I mean, it's been his first name for twelve years. That's long enough, now that I think about it. I'm sure Luke will agree."

"I'm sure he will," I said, wrapping my fingers around my druthers.

"And—silly me! Why didn't I think of this in the first place? Dad—*you* should pick his middle name," my daughter exclaimed.

"Me?" I said.

"Oh, yes! That would be wonderful! Billy—I mean, George would be so proud to have you select his middle name."

"Well," I said, pondering for a moment, "my middle name's Hubert. Do you think he'd like that?"

After a beat, my daughter said, "Hubert! Of course! Why didn't I think of that? Oh, he'll be thrilled! Thanks, Dad. You're the best!"

"Just trying to help," I said. By this time my phone was lighting up with other calls. "Listen, Hon, I gotta go. We can talk more about this tomorrow. But before I hang up, let me leave you with a little thought. Have you ever considered using that hyphenated maiden name thing? Funk-Giovanni has a nice ring to it, don't you think?"

"Dad, you're a genius!" my daughter said.

I hung up. Two incoming call numbers flashed on my screen. One I recognized as my ex-wife's lawyer. The other was from Rob McIntyre. Which call should I take first?

I looked at my druthers. It looked at me. "This one's on you, little man," it said.

Zzzt!
"It is our indifference to ideas that we did not suspect." --Louis Aragon

The gypsies in the next room who spoke
a language you didn't understand have
loaded their caravan and departed for their
homeland behind an obsidian mountain,
where it is always twilight and the Wi-Fi signal's
lost and the tavern lights have always just come on,
where the jukebox alternates between
hits from The Summer of '74, and the girl
at the end of the bar with her hair tied back
in a yellow scarf smiles as she watches another
moth fly into the bug zapper which for some reason
is painted pink and has your name on it.

Come Out of the Rain, Gray Bird

I don't have a theory of literature—at least not one that sticks.

I push words in wheelbarrows no one depends on.

I'm prone to whims.

Terms like "chalice," "somnambulist," "parallax," "aleatory," and "orphanage"—I mean "orchid" dazzle me unduly.

I can point to Orion in the night sky, but it's hard to live by myths when all you remember is a belt and a scabbard. You, on the other hand, claim to be able to point him out in daylight.

You are also quick to tell me that I dream with one eye open. This raises many questions:

Do you know that the catbird mimics and rearranges the songs of other birds into a longer song of its own?

Did you know that every face one sees in dreams is a composite of faces seen in waking life—that no dream face is entirely invented?

Also, why do my watchbands keep breaking?

Will this rain ever stop?

Why did you always live on the top floor?

Why can't I see my hand in front of my purely invented face?

Finally, will any of these questions lead to a theory of literature?

It's time to carry the load, to close my inner eye, to pluck the devil out of every detail.

It's time for us to engage in a meaningful dialectic. I could do it alone, but it might take a lifetime—and then some!

Or we could wait till the rain stops—and then some!

We could seduce a thought, caulk a notion, batten down a prevarication—and then some!

The point is, you look like someone I know, even though you appear only to my inner eye.

Perhaps you find me interesting.

Perhaps you would like to read my story.

Perhaps then you could tell me which parent I most resemble—and I could tell you how many faces your face is made of.

: Is

: is leading us past a surrealist painter's horizon
with its broken statuary and liquid clocks,
its febrile light and kite-shadows : is
bringing about by sheer force
an unwanted reconcilement of opposites
on a muddy plain : is felt in the brain as
an imagined buoyancy whose biological function,
while certain, remains unknown
: is a necklace of black beads worn by Death's mistress,
who is still waiting for him to come home : is the
ubiquity of proud flesh : is how you mistake
your lover's pleading for chamber music :
is the way eternal Beauty requires an object in time : is the
story of a man who heard a cricket in the cathedral
and searched for it, obsessively but without success,
till his dying day : is the paradox of memory,
binding us to time by pretending to stand outside of it :
is that moment toward dusk when the sea turns to
liquid mercury, brighter than the sky : is a blind
buzzard circling a stone : is an unbridgeable gap,
like that between a musical score and its performance,
or between "I" and the one who says it: is the sum total
of what's possible to forget: is a null set: is festooned:
:is in parentheses: is trying to imagine reproduction by
mitosis—what forms of desire it involves, what pain,
what pleasure, what kind of poetry it inspires—and whether
this might be preferable: is a gold pocket watch molting
in a palace of crystal: is seeing words as fireflies in an
opaque darkness: is a map site, silent regarding its accuracy:
is the gate through which an intruder may enter: is the
source of proverbs: is not wishing to bestir itself: is keeping
quiet and letting time do its work: is willingly suspending
belief on strings so as to manipulate it from above: is
learning to speak in epitaphs: is embracing postponements:
is remembering that blood and thought, while necessary for

each other, must remain in conflict: is refusing to be squeezed
by allegory: is finding a way to repress certain memories while
still remaining aware of the repression: is learning to speak
from the heart, using memorized lines: is standing before a
mirror and asking yourself "What do I misrecognize?": is a
ceiling fan, barely turning: is something seen that we cannot name—
wingless angels, vague potencies, the world outside ourselves,
unremembered dreams, boundless seas in whose depths
unimaginable creatures make their own light: is shouting "I"
and listening for echoes

Colloquy on Metaphor as a Universal Solvent

The keynote speaker drove a red truck through the proceedings.

A panel of dignitaries planted crown vetch in the audience's cerebrums.

Fish scales were awarded to prehensile recipients.

A slide presentation molted before our eyes, causing some to ovulate.

The Master of Ceremonies noted the astringent qualities of astrological charts from 17th century Goo Gai Pan.

Clog dancers were summarily executed.

Most of our transitive verbs developed blisters.

"Literally" was our universal safe word.

Phallic symbols were checked in with hats and coats.

Strip dancers, some Aristotelian, some Platonic, formed nimbus clouds on stage.

Small groups were assigned to polish jig-saw puzzles, coagulate, ween thistles, and lick rusty cheese graters.

A union representative dispensed trowels.

The presiding officer married a blue heron to a red herring in an Andalusian tea ceremony, replete with bladderwort conflagrations.

Resurgent tendinitis gripped us all.

August

Come August, the tiger lilies have written their memoirs.
Every day is a wide-eyed stare. Blacktop sealers
stir buckets of tar and dream about the Pleiades.
Beneath the web of cricket song, night's
whispered questions link us in a single dream.
An old woman brings berries in a porcelain bowl.
Her crazy husband counts shadows, giving them
biblical names: Gershom, Belshazzar, Abaddon.
A stranger in a raincoat enters the convenience store
and proclaims himself a prophet. The night clerk
feels something stirring behind her eye-patch.
A voice on the gospel station shouts, over and over,
"Who shall wake the brakeman?" The moon
sends down its bitter, ineffectual light.

Third Party

The candidates held a debate in Union Hall. I arrived late, just as the opening statements were winding down, so I decided to wend my way as close to the front as I could.

"Everyone knows I gilded the lily," Candidate A was saying. "But many don't know that I also gilded the trillium." A wave of applause rippled through the crowd. "And if given a chance, I'll gild geraniums, too!"

The applause swelled. Someone behind me shouted "Down to the roots!" and the people around him cheered. Half the crowd began to chant "Down to the roots! Down to the roots!" Caught up in the moment, I chanted, too.

The candidate smiled. "To the roots!" he said.

All this time, Candidate B stood behind the podium shaking his head. He wore a faint smirk. When the chant died down, he raised a hand and said, "Someone's been frying when he should have been baking." He waited while a few people tittered. "And that means—"here he paused dramatically—"no one's ready when it's time to baste!" There was a whoop in the back of the room. As if on cue, a number of people began waving "Time to Baste" signs. I could feel the excitement building as I pushed forward. Two rows ahead me, I spied an attractive woman, so I wormed my way closer to her. "I've counted the vapor trails," Candidate B went on, his voice rising. "I've reconfigured the non-Euclidean origami and watched yeast rise in the City of Enoch."

"And still you calibrated!" the woman, now beside me, shouted. She smiled broadly and placed a hand over her heart.

"Calibrated indeed!" the candidate shouted. "Calibrated and read all the gauges! Some people say I should shepherd exegetes, but I tell you right now—and I dare my opponent to deny it: quintessences and lapidary undertakings don't mix!" The room erupted. A few boos rang out, but most of the crowd jumped up and down, cheering wildly. I had to admit, it was contagious. The woman beside me wore a look of rapture.

"How about that?" I said to her.

"When he speaks, it's like a star bath," she said. "He awakens the needful dust in us all."

"I can feel mine awakening," I said, inching closer. I noticed she was wearing one of Candidate B's buttons on her ample bosom. "He's right about those exegetes," I added.

Just then, candidate A stepped out from behind his podium and approached the lip of the stage. He put his hands on his hips and let his gaze sweep across the rows of people. The crowd, anticipating his response, grew quiet. "Friends," he said at last, "my opponent knows as much about quintessences as a Texas twister.

"How's that?" someone yelled.

The candidate smiled. "I'll tell you," he said. "He's like a Texas twister because he spins and spins and he kicks up a little dust, but he never makes it to the gravy junction. He's just an echo in a pie pan."

Some people applauded while others jeered. The woman next to me screamed, "He could spit in your tureen!"

The candidate ignored her and began to prowl the stage. "Friends, I'm not here to tell you what you want to hear," he said. "I'm here to tell you that no one uses sorrel, then climbs the monkey bars. There's such a thing as subcutaneous hoodwinks, and it's time my opponent gilds his own confabulations!"

The crowd exploded. Some folks gave each other high fives, while others shouted indignantly. The woman beside me was apoplectic. "You banshee-jacker. You nylon-run!" she screamed. I watched her jumping up and down. This debate is going well, I thought, jumping beside her to show my empathy.

"Friends!" Candidate A shouted, removing his jacket, "you can't lasso a zephyr with a garden hose!" Pandemonium was breaking out. Candidate B now approached the front of the stage and began to say something, but he couldn't outshout the crowd. Soon both candidates were standing toe to toe, screaming at each other. I couldn't hear what they were saying, but I saw their veins bulging.

The woman beside me was screaming, "You dissolute custard mop!"

I leaned in close and yelled in her ear. "Candidate A doesn't deserve the time of day! Let's go have a drink and plan his political ruin. I know a good place a few blocks from here."

The woman looked at me and frowned. "I couldn't do that."

"Why not?" I said, hoping to ride the momentum of the moment. "We can start a grassroots movement."

"I'm afraid I couldn't," she said. "He's my husband."

"What?" I said, confused. "Haven't you been rooting for Candidate B all this time?"

"Yes," she said. "I prefer his policies. His positions will do the most people the most good. I even find him more attractive. That's why I'm his mistress. But I must remain politically loyal to my husband, who rescued me from the backwoods country, brought me to the city, and made me what I am today."

"And what's that?" I asked.

"Someone who, as of this moment, is done talking to you," she said.

Lake Reverie

Someone built a dam on the river of regret.

It transformed the landscape, submerging the old castles, the charnel houses, and the churches.

The villagers were relocated.

After a time, new trees grew around the lake's perimeter. A species of bird not yet identified now inhabits them. You've never seen one, but its cry can cause your heart to skip a beat.

When you and other villagers returned to the lake, you became aware of its special properties.

Staring at the water in moonlight makes permeable the veil between waking and dreaming. These effects are permanent. Perhaps this is because nowhere else on earth does the sky reflect water.

For this reason, swimming, while inevitable, is not recommended.

Signs around the lake expressly forbid ice fishing. In the early years, a number of villagers ventured out on the frozen surface to drop lines above their drowned childhood homes. Immobilized by nostalgia, they could not be persuaded to return. Spring thaw claimed them.

Of course, the lake invites you to contemplate its fish, moving like silver punctuation marks through its dark pages. But you must supply the words.

Do not attempt to put out fires with this water.

Do not come near when the lake is feeding.

Likewise, if you hear what you think is singing, never try to hum along.

Do not drink here if the world is still your friend.

Come Again Another Day

While you crocheted splints for the wounded,
I was chasing an idea for a poem. It had tapped
me on the shoulder that morning, and when I turned,
it giggled and ran off. I chased it through Luxembourg
and Lichtenstein. I pursued it across the Dardanelles,
where Lord Byron is said to have swum in May of 1810.
Next, I tracked it to a backwoods road near Numidia,
Pennsylvania, site of a meaningless but tenacious childhood
memory. I was a deer in its tail lights, yet I felt myself
drawing closer. You, meanwhile, were making poultices
for stutterers and frostbite victims, serving humanity with
the sort of distinction for which few adjectives suffice.
I gave up on the poem. I went to the kitchen and peeled
an apple, pondering my human failings. It was raining,
and had been for as long as I could remember—long enough
to wash all color from the birds. Now most of them were
translucent gray, more shadow than substance, their songs
luted into sad vespers. I put down the apple and watched
a strange insect crawling up my doorframe. How to describe it?
I'd never seen one before: oblong, swarthy, and concupiscent,
yet with a priest-like demeanor, and maybe facile, too. . . .
Oh, none of those words seemed right! No wonder I couldn't
write a poem! How could I, when the words dropped like beads
from a necklace and scattered on the floor like, like, roaches
scattering from the light? Ugh. And there you were, sucking the
poison from dog bite victims! How could I compete? I'd lost my
poem, so I took a picture of the insect and posted it on social media:
"Does anybody know the name of this?" Rain fell from the eaves.
My apple turned brown. You phoned me between cholera patients
to remind me that the ancient city of Troy was located on the
Dardanelles—maybe I could use that in my poem. "It's been done,"
I said. "Well, then, did you know that King Xerxes once sentenced
the Dardanelles to 300 lashes?" "He actually had the water
whipped?" I asked. "Yes. After a storm destroyed a bridge
he'd built at Hellespont, he ordered the engineers beheaded
and commanded his soldiers to flog the water." "How did that

work out?" I said. I was about to make a more clever remark
when a burst of coughing came over the phone. "Who's that?"
"They just brought in three ambulances full of fever dream victims.
I have to go," you said. You hung up. I felt sheepish for your
dragging up the whole Dardanelles business again. I'd tried to crop
it out earlier, but I clung to the hope that relaying it in your voice
later in the poem might make it relevant. Instead, all I'd done was
pull you away from more important duties, like mixing powdered
gruel and applying leeches to bunions. Still, what about my verbal
aphasia? When would you get around to curing *me*, or at least
alleviating my symptoms? I sat in my armchair, determined to
write a poem. I tried to make my brain a construction site. I
watched the words parading past, some of them peripatetic, some
prehensile. None wore protective goggles. None was licensed to
operate heavy machinery. All were dripping wet from this damnable
rain. I could feel myself becoming translucent. My phone chirped,
but I couldn't move. The sound of rain seemed to fill the house
with static. I clutched the armrests as if they were the sides of
a lifeboat. Maybe they were. My phone chirped again. I glanced
at the screen and saw seven identical messages. "Do I even have
seven friends?" I asked myself. All of the messages said "It's an earwig."

Dei ex Machinis

Father, in his flying pulpit, touches down on a cindered plain. "Why aren't
you in the chancel?" he asks, as though someone is there to hear him. Oh wait,
maybe it's me. I've just finished strapping the word "beatitude" to a gurney,
and of course I'm wielding a bicycle pump. It's embarrassing to be caught red-
handed like this, but Father appears not to notice. He's wearing his darkest robe
and a purple stole. His clerical collar blinks on and off. When he speaks, his
voice is like a boat's wake smoothed over: "I bequeath you one absence and
three blueprints, though what the blueprints depict is also invisible," he says.
What am I supposed to do with *that*? Before I can ask, he launches into the
sky, returning to his fitful orbit, leaving me to tame my urgencies by myself.
And that's a problem—my one good eye sees what it wants to see. Was he
really here? Were his words meant for me or for himself? How was I supposed
to feel? Could anyone say? Sometimes innuendo's shadows have shadows of
their own, all even-toothed and ready to comb out the night's tresses, or so I
imagine. Of course, I've been chewing daffodils, whose deleterious effects are
well documented. I turn back to "beatitude." Was it time to attach the bicycle
pump? It was. "This will hurt me more than it hurts you," I say, but it isn't true.
I attach the nozzle to the letter "i" and begin to pump: *pfft! pfft! pfft! pfft! pfft!*
With each influx of air, "beatitude" swells until its golden skin turns translucent
and I can see its veins stretching taut. It looks ready to burst. "This will be
better than last time," I say. The last word I did this to was "logocentric."
It put up a good fight, but in the end it succumbed, as they all do. And the
mess—well, I'm sure you can imagine! How thankful I was when the silver
birds came and picked the ground clean! "It's a sign of something," I said,
and, though I could not say what, I felt vindicated-- even when the dark ladder
appeared and the only way was down.

Fourth Session

Dispatch from the Hinterlands

The bad news from the front is that there is no front.
Someone left the gate open; the fighting stopped
before it started; now everyone's sated and just wants to sleep.
The translators are drunk; they've forgotten which language
is their native tongue, and so, as the saying goes, "The boll weevil
lies with the skink." Now both sides wear blue blazers by choice.
The new national anthem sounds like indigestion set to music,
especially by the thirteenth verse—the one where the gods
instruct man on the use of gunpowder—but we go on singing anyway.
Have we taken control of our feelings at last? Shall we wear numbness
like a crown? These are, of course, the wrong questions,
which is why they spring so easily to mind. Likewise, the need
for a dour prophet and a list of jeremiads seems obvious in times
such as these, and therefore should not be trusted. When will a
beardless youth clad in gold raiment descend from the mountain
and proclaim, "Hey folks! Doing just fine! Carry on!" Never, and
such wishes blur our mythologies. But this, too, shall pass. Tomorrow
we can visit the Leader's peacock farm and there determine
if it's a treaty or a charter we want. Afterwards, maybe dinner
and a show. If all goes well, we can "trust but verify" all night long,
and report our "victory" back home to the sad little man at headquarters.

In the Nutty Pith of a Quandary, I Make My Stand

Conflagration of geraniums
like an old man's thoughts—
words open like smiling bivalves—
catbirds fly from mirrors
into intentionalities of frost,
the same way you succumb
to latencies of violet, left-handed,
without a second look.
Comic meteors, obtuse catcalls,
Persian carpets of well-read desire—
how fitting your garlands! How apt
your itching monocles! Aimless
apostrophes—like ghosts rising
from the sofa, seen peripherally—
refuse to tarry. They've built
an apothecary shop on the corner
of my eye. Sleeping dogs guard nothing,
so the saying goes, but atop the hill
the hound's eye opens. It is yellow,
sees time in black and white, wants to fix us
in the vestibule of its gaze.
Who, then, will reclaim our image?
Who, then, will sing like sad curlews
on love's fractal shores?

The Quarry

At night's apogee, our words became autumn leaves--
brilliant but falling. My hands became door-to-door salesmen.
Someone was tickling my phantom pain; the least slip of a knife
can leave a trail of unwanted consequences, as well we know.
What emerged next was a series of tendencies shaped like a
debutante's tiara, but set at a jaunty angle, like a gangster's fedora.
I'll never forget the sight of a half-moon floating above the
limestone quarry—the way it failed to illuminate your eyes, while
flattening the occasion into a wan fresco. If I told you that it filled me
with a preternatural ennui, would you believe me? Memory's a
dead-end street, after all, and what I want to know now is
"How do I know that all I see, and therefore feel, isn't a result of a
stigmatism, real or imagined?" Beans in a pot, a lump under the sheets,
the way frost forms a fern leaf on my window—doubt all of it!
Perhaps I should have been a haberdasher or the guy who works
the movie projector. At least then I'd have the respect of my colleagues.
Oh well. I've leased my memories and you've leased yours. Or leashed.
Did I mention they filled the quarry with water fifty years ago?
Apparently they'd mined all they could. Still, despite the fence
and warning signs, kids have been drowning there ever since.

Threnody for an Hourglass

A dollar becomes a fool's spleen
on a salver; a grandfather clock suffers
ennui beyond permissible boundaries,
cursing pigeons and accordion music
from a park bench. An hourglass wishes to take up
cross-country skiing like a good suburbanite,
but it lives indoors and owns no sweater
patterned in chevrons or fleur-di-lis.
At five, the bank's vault doors close with a crocodile hiss;
the tellers say their secret mass;
their deity is a bell-ringer's apparatus,
but the clapper has run away
and left no forwarding address.
Now digital clocks on every corner
stack the hours like poker chips
and weigh the nation's guilt for all to see.
This makes the depositors restless.
"Bring back the mechanical sun dial!"
they shout, and the administrators, whose open,
black umbrellas resemble gargoyles' mouths
gaping in astonishment, echo their cries.
But it is too late. All of the mechanical sun-dials
have been tossed in the sea and left to fate.
Some float like confetti on the green waves.
Others sink down and down,
past mermaids and festive fish,
into the dark pituitary of a sleeping god.

Watching Myself Write a Poem Is Like Staring At My Fingers While Playing Piano

Rain turns to snow as the season's key modulates.
Shall I compare you to March 23, 2019?
I'm trying to get more specificity into my poems.
I say "No ideas but in flywheels," though your
fuel-to-air ratio of flame reminds me of our old
Tirrill Bunsen burner—upon which our derangement
of sense and so much more depended. Some called it
an "objective correlative," but you knew the score.
Stop paraphrasing! For once, try to *be*—not *mean*.
And don't give me the goo-goo eyes! My nightingale talks
in its sleep—so what? Nothing to get all "Thomas Hardy" about!
A child asks me "What is the Bermuda grass rhizome?"
I point out that the European larch is the best-loved deciduous
conifer in the world. He's not impressed. "Okay, then," I tell him.
"This sentence will be thirteen syllables exactly."
I wave my hand with a magician's flourish, then add
"Did you know that most New Formalists drive Mazdas?"
"This poem is destined to fail in its ontological striving,"
the child tells me. It is still snowing. The woods are filling up.
Have you ordered your transcription factor staining buffer sets
or your cell lysis and preservation assays? How about those
magnetic cell isolation beads? There's a god no one's heard of
whose name is something unpronounceable spelled backwards
and who prays to us unceasingly in a language we cannot hear,
much less understand. If I were a L-A-N-G-U-A-G-E poet,
I'd explain it to you. Syntax is politics. Everyone was surprised
when it snowed before noon. Now I wait for the plow man
with my team of black hounds. Above the clouds, the sky is
streaked with meteors and the blood of angels. Everything is
burning. I am burning. You are more lovely and more temperate.

The Passenger

October's gray-needled rain
pelts the windshield. The driver
hasn't spoken, and it occurs to me
that I haven't seen his face—just
two dark eyes in the rearview.
But when I look for his license,
I find nothing. We're speeding
through a part of the city I've never
seen before, taking corners a little too
fast. The tires hiss like snakes on the wet
macadam. "Turn your wipers on," I say.
"How can you see like that?"
"I can see," he says. "Can you?"
I look out the window. The signs
on the buildings are in a language I
don't recognize. And the buildings
themselves are peculiar—oddly angled
—as if their architect designed them in
his sleep. "Where are we?" I ask.
The eyes in the rearview lock onto mine.
"Halfway there," the driver says.
"Halfway where?" I say.
"Exactly," he says.

Don't Touch That Dial

Aided and abetted by the tourism of your affection,
I sought the artificial rose that dreamed you into being.
Wrong! Someone kept twisting the radio dial—station
bleeding into station, static in between, everything fleeting.

"I am not a melancholic!" she cried, hurling her nosegay
to the Persian rug her Uncle Loomis brought home
from the war. A skid in need of greasing, a bouquet
of evasions, her speech meandered through a thicket

of "sweet spots." Was this, at last, the New Poem?
Should we tend to the serpents in the garden, Maria?
They coil amidst the rutabagas, threatening to strike.
It's all done with computer graphics and satellites,

for which we're billed monthly. And the hegemonic
vicissitudes of middle management render us numb,
thus assisting our self-amputation. "We hate it, too,
but we're getting pressure from above." Above?

Not according to Dante, though we've opened new
northern sea routes, thanks to global warming. Shall we
descend to the engine room of language and tinker with
the gauges? Gerunds could change the world, unraveling

our sexual parataxis by allaying its psalmic undertones. Did
you catch the weather report as it flashed by? What is this
palimpsest of interference that complicates my dictation?
The New Poem is brought to you by Geico. The quality of mercy

is not strain'd. Some stations only come in at night. Wake up,
everybody! Wake up! Something is killing the artificial rose.
"It was the paprika!" Detective Willoughby exclaimed, eliciting
a gasp from the kitchen crew. Will my love ever cease

in its power to appall? Will someone sing beneath the
candied moon? Will corporate barons invent new forms
of confetti? Can anyone remember our call letters?
This is only a test, Maria, mein liebchen. Don't stay tuned.

For Subcutaneous Use Only

The promised relief, dispensed by doves, never came. Still, I celebrated the arrival of another dawn, poking its gray fingers through the blinds like articles of faith. I'd reached a stage in life where everything needed to be pared down. Feelings, perceptions, notions—all of it. For too long I'd ridden bareback in the mannequin factory, stirring the multi-colored goulash, as they say. But now my excitability came at a cost.

One thing I knew: there was a color to which all of us were blind, though it pervaded everything. But it was no longer the object of my search. The very thought of it exacerbated my symptoms. My body had become a puppet too heavy for its strings. The interstices I'd loved to trace had grown wider—and fuzzier. Maybe they weren't interstices at all.

So the question became: "Pared down to what?"

"A stone's catechism" was the only answer I could think of.

I closed my eyes and whispered "cantus firmus" three times. It was a trick Aunt Lizzie taught me when I was but a child. When I opened my eyes, the Virgin Mary stood before me, holding a pen and spiral-bound notebook. "What rhymes with 'supercilious'?" she asked.

While I thought of an answer, I observed tiny cherubim circling above her head. Then, just before I could say "This soup is bilious," I realized that the cherubs were actually pigeons painted pink. Their cooing gave them away. "Hey, you! The jig is up!" I shouted.

"Drat!" the Virgin Mary said. Instantly she transformed back into a ficus plant. The pigeons dispersed. A nurse stood by the foot of the bed, saying "I can't make any sense of your chart."

Heinous Apogee of Reflexive Scribbling

Someone hands you a facsimile—of what, you aren't sure.

Read it later! Right now it's time for *ideas*!

Say it's Friday and overcast. The constabularies have accused another prophet of filing a false report, though he maintains that the future hasn't happened yet and therefore they have no evidence against him. He pleads his case by extending an analogy. "Every thought leaves a slime trail," he says, "but it's only seen to glisten in certain kinds of light. Whether you can see it depends on what kind of light you bring. Are you a moon in June? A glow-worm? A menorah? Perhaps you're an aurora or St. Elmo's fire? Are you a love letter burning in the parking lot? Are you a light at the end of the tunnel?"

"What's your point?" the constables say, readying their night sticks.

"My point," says the prophet, "is that if you are always high noon in Albuquerque, then that slime trail will vanish in the white-hot bleach of your gaze. You'll never see the path it makes in the dark. You'll never see the dark."

The beating that follows bespeaks the prophet's place in society.

Is it martyrdom if no one complains?

Is the facsimile in your hand a "reasonable" one? Perhaps you're a facsimile, too?

Say it's Friday. The sky is etch-a-sketch gray. Is it true that narrative—or even a grammatically correct sentence—implies an ideology? What about the deliberate disruption of narrative, a favorite ploy of the disaffected? Has that become a tired trick as well?

"When you write," she said, "do you begin with certain themes in mind?"

This happened three weeks ago. Your immediate reaction was to laugh and shake your head before uttering an emphatic "No!" Then, realizing this might appear arrogant, you choke back that response and patiently explain that you most often began with an image, a metaphor, a phrase or puzzling scenario, then wrote to find out what it meant—or what it didn't mean. "If I begin with a theme, the writing becomes too easily paraphraseable," you told her. "And if that's the case, why bother to write it?"

"But aren't you afraid all that discontinuity will lose your audience?" she asked.

You wanted to say "What audience?" Instead, you explained, as tactfully as you could, that what mattered was to create a waking dream, not a thesis. You wanted a structure of words that defamiliarized the quotidian, not mere window dressing of commonplaces. "Hopefully an audience will find its way there eventually," you said.

This conversation is a memory. Time can be expanded and compressed in a narrative. The ancients believed in circular time—a series of cycles in which key events repeated themselves like a sunrise. Yet other traditions, like the Hebrews', involved a linear conception of time, in which a sequence of events led from genesis to apocalypse. Is it time to read your facsimile? Is that what this is leading to? Why have you put off doing so? Is your deferral a structural device, a way of creating narrative unity in an otherwise disjointed text?

Say it's Friday. A pewter sky. You're watching a documentary on Michelangelo, whose sculpture you admire but whose Sistine Chapel paintings disturb you—all those over-muscled characters looking like they'd been stuffed with mattresses, prototypes of today's comic book superheroes but hardly realistic—unless you believe that Jesus was a pro wrestler on steroids. Where is the proportional beauty one sees in his statue of David? Clearly, Michelangelo knew the difference and therefore he must have chosen to distort the Sistine figures. But why? Was he merely creating Christian propaganda-- making Biblical characters seem larger than life? Every image of the body implies an ideology. The same could be said for every landscape, every still life. [Music, too, is not exempt—those abstract sounds plucked from the air and shaped according to principles of harmony and rhythm may seem "universal" but are in fact culturally determined. Think of the "blue notes" in African music, so unsettling to the European ear. Think of the freight they carry when the two cultures collide.]

Think of the facsimile in your hand. How do you even know it's a facsimile if you haven't read it yet? Because this text began with that assertion, like a "given" in a mathematical proof? Would any of these verbal meanderings be different if the idea of a facsimile never appeared? To what extent does the "framing device" of the facsimile affect one's reading—or writing—of the text? To what extent does the fact it's Friday and the sky is one great cataract shape the reader's interpretation? Is this text in fact a series of paraphraaseable themes, despite the author's disdain for such writing? Is there too much high noon in Albuquerque? Is it time for more disruption?

Suppose the mirror coughed up blood this morning.

Suppose the mind could not think of itself in second person. Would it be time to take my stigmata for a walk? To set the grackles free?

How can I sneak my unrequiting lover into yet another text—perhaps disguised as a "somebody" who places a "facsimile" in my hand?

Has anybody got the time?

Some names are marble on the tongue, others broken glass.

She had the look of someone who stared through microscopes for a living.

Wind over flower, wind over stone.

The facsimile is blank and getting blanker.

Here, you read it.

I'll be collecting memento mori for the next shortage.

Prattling at the Cold Cup Café

Do contemporary poets still write at cafes? I don't see how. The chirpy people at the next table won't shut up. How can I hear my voices over their voices? They're reciting *Reader's Digest* articles aloud, grooming imaginary poodles for the Gated Community Dog Show, and reliving last summer's bring-your-own-surprise-casserole patio dinner party.

What to do?

There will be no supernatural intervention.

I count 364 days until the next Ides of March. Everyone's awaiting platitudinous spring, clenching sprigs of pussy willow in their teeth. Me? I want to do away with the Lyrical I, or at least usher him to a guest room where the door locks on both sides. He gets unruly when the sun goes down. He's been baptized in chamomile; his cologne smells like Tintern Abbey used to on garbage day. Through the closed door, he tells me he's composing *Nacht Musik for Zither and Theremin.* Oh boy! In *that* sleep what dreams may come? It's got me wishing transubstantiation was consensual.

I'll bet these people go home and binge-watch the apocalypse while nibbling cucumber sandwiches on cauliflower flat bread crisps. I'm picturing them in their living room, playing Parcheesi. There's a copy of Nietzsche's *Will To Power* on the shelf; it's been gathering dust for sixteen years, with a bookmark still on page 33. Oh well, it doesn't matter. Zarathustra's an Uber driver now.

What else are the voices saying?

The world is better off because some of us are cowards.

You can buy lapis lazuli on Amazon.

There's an essential oil for every malady, save poor command of syntax, and a how-to book for every form of spiritual cleansing, with or without phosphates.

Is belief in ideology ideological? If you were a flower, what kind of flower would you be?

There's a self for every way of speaking, but who is the self who leaps between them?

Stop pounding the door! Some of us are trying to sleep! I have to cultivate seven deep images by morning.

I wish the Objective Correlative Store was open.

The word of the day is "bouffant."

No, it's "cantilever."

Stop pounding the door! I can't hear my selves think!

It takes years of training and a commitment to asceticism in order to master the Theremin. Did you know its vibrations are affected by moonlight and stained glass? Did you know that its invention was foretold years ago in a dream of Pythagoras? Of course, some things should never be written down. It's true! Sometimes I stop thinking, but the words go on without me. Once you know this, it's easier to spot the skid marks.

Stop pounding the door! Minerva, bring me an aspirin—it feels like my head's exploding.

Must all Theremins be played in the Phrygian mode?

I haven't had coffee this cold since my Baltic vacation. That's pretty much all I remember from that trip—cold coffee, and a little shop in Darlowo that sold children's handprints in plaster and silhouette portraits of the dead.

Anyway, my cup is empty. It's time for an ending. Here are seven to choose from.

1. The bell above the café door rings. In flows a girl with an elegant bouffant and a figure to cantilever any man's heart. She passes me without looking, and my coffee heats up. She goes to the counter and orders an espresso. As she parts her lips for the first sip, the lock on the guest room door shatters, and the Lyrical I bursts free, waving his stigmata and shouting "Isn't it pretty to think so?"

2. One of the silhouette portraits of the dead bore a striking resemblance to Uncle Yazmin—so much so, that I felt the need to call him and make sure he was still alive. What a relief when he answered the phone! "I can't believe you called!" he said. "I have wonderful news! I received a letter from my long lost twin brother, Ludvies. We were separated at birth because of the war, but he found me! I thought he was dead, but tomorrow he's catching the train from Luxemburg and coming to see me!" I glanced at the dark silhouette and noted yesterday's date on the bottom corner. "I wouldn't get your hopes up," I said.

3. Stop pounding the door! I wish these voices could sing in unison. No I don't. It's just that the zithers feel neglected, and who can blame them? Yet played in a minor key on the night of the new moon, they attract more moths than candlelight.

4. One of the people at the next table turned to me. He waited until I met his gaze. Then he said, "Excuse me, sir. I know it's none of our business, but we were wondering: why are you wearing a sackcloth?"

5. The interested reader is advised to search the following phrases on the Internet: "cafes and writing," "Polish legend of the pussy willow," "Nietzsche's madness," "powers of lapis lazuli," "funniest looking flower," "how does a cantilever suspension work," "'lyrical I' vs. narrator," and "Russian espionage and electromagnetic fields: the story of the Theremin." The interested writer is invited to use these phrases as prompts for a story of twelve hundred words or less.

6. "No! I'm the one locking *you* out!" screamed the Lyrical I from behind the guest room door.

7. Then Karla came to a stark realization. The inflection in Gunther's voice, imperceptible to all but her, made it clear: he did not love her—not in the way she needed to be loved. For though he had shown her kindness, though he had treated her deferentially, though, indeed, his face glowed when he was in her company and they shared many joys and pastimes, he was not willing—or maybe not capable—of responding to her need for solace and reassurance and tender ministrations. If anything, he seemed to shrink from her whenever she expressed those needs, whenever she came too close. She sat with her hands folded, pretending to listen as he played the recorder. She noted the mask of concentration, the closed eyes and furrowed brow, as he drew the music from

some place deep inside himself. She wanted to map that place. She wanted him to look at *her* as he played, as if to say "This cantata is for you, and you alone!" But that was not to be. She saw now for the first time that, in his eyes, her need was cloying, a sign of weakness, something that would drain him, spur his resentment, and ultimately drive him away. For this reason, he would never share that part of him from whence the music came. He would never bare his soul—not for her, not ever. Karla turned toward the window so her tears could not be seen. It was a beautiful evening: the village lights twinkled in the valley as though mirroring the stars above, while through the bare branches of the sycamore the orphaned, heretical moon spread its stolen light.

The Exploding Clock

I always meant to tell you how it feels, crawling on all fours in Room 17 of The Palm Motel, searching for tiny clock parts. There must be hundreds of them sprinkled across this muskrat-colored rug. Finding them all seems impossible—but without them, I have no story.

What you should know is this: the clock exploded sometime in the night. Of course, I can't say exactly when because I have no other timepiece for a reference. I can't even say which night. All I know is that the clock split open when I wasn't looking and scattered its contents—tiny springs, gears, fly-wheels, and mechanisms known only to clock makers—like so much confetti across this mammalian carpet. And I can't check out until the clock is reassembled.

Perhaps I should take stock, if not for my sake then for yours. Why have I returned to this two-star motel in my hometown? I can't think of a reason. All of my relatives are either dead or moved away. I have no friends here. Up until I became stuck in this room, I led a peripatetic life, the residual effects of which are only partially known. True, I've never been commended for my moral turpitude—my salivary glands don't function properly, and this gives rise to misinterpretations of my character. But if I may be the judge, I'm not an unethical person, except for certain obsessive fantasies to which I sometimes return.

This is why having the promise of you to talk to feels so important.

Shall I describe this scene for you? It's hard to settle on the significant details. First the town. I could tell you that we're on the county's edge. I could tell you about the sickeningly sweet breeze from the marmalade factory, or how on August nights like this the air is itchy with cricket song .I could tell you how everything here is a sinkhole waiting to happen. Then there's this room. What is there to say? Four bare walls, a curtained window beyond which the Vacancy sign crackles and hums, a lumpy bed, and this awful carpet that feeds on the residuum of previous guests. Someone has scrawled their exegesis in the margins of the Gideon bible: what begins as verbal notes turns into mathematical formulae before terminating abruptly in Leviticus.

Somehow all of this seems beside the point. At least I think so. How can there be a "point" outside of time? I'll never know until the clock is reassembled. Until then, there's only this room, this gerund in which searching is ongoing. Each glint of light in the rug could be part of the puzzle. Of course, I haven't the vaguest notion how to construct a clock. How will I know when I've found all the pieces? What if I don't have the proper tools? What if I lack exactitude? How can I, suspended in time, engage in a sequence of steps whose order is paramount? And if I succeed—does that bring me closer to you, or does it push us further apart? After all, you once lived here, too.

So I keep on crawling, sifting through carpet fibers, looking for light specks, hoping someday I'll be telling you this. Otherwise, I'll just be telling time.

The Gaze

Dusk hangs its dirty linens. Time to gargle. Three pills. There are those who will return your gaze, but they are few. Change your bandage. Wash your hair. Eat your soup—it facilitates dreams and helps to spread these wildflowers. The idea of a lawn seems preposterous. The idea of a lawn seems absurd. Two pills. The moon won't return your gaze. You mustn't stare, or they'll know what you're thinking. (Notice I didn't say "they'll know what you *mean*." Wait— who am *I*? Am I you? Am I how you see yourself? Am I your shadow, your constant companion, or do I exist only within these parentheses?)

Torsos of alabaster, torsos of marble. Time to gargle. The night is wound in barbed wire. You live in the whorls of a deaf god's ear. Does another return your gaze? Does another lick its lips? Already it's a long winter. Something is eluded. Don't stare. Three pills. Dream your soup. The idea of a lawn is nearly impossible. And if another knows your thoughts? Torso of moonlight—and a word like "luminous," repeated aloud, becomes a strange gelatin in somebody's mouth. The night brings its fears, its salts. One pill. (I am here, waiting.) Have vespers begun? The lamplighter has gone to sleep. You wait in the hall; you wait in the mezzanine. And now the night lies coiled about your feet, coiled like the whorls of a deaf god's ear. Humming stars. Wash your hair. Torsos of bronze turn green in time.

Five pills. Already it's a long winter. Crisscrossing shadows—kiss them while they're sleeping. Wrap them in barbed wire, or else they'll know what you're thinking. Torsos of glass shatter if you love them. Change your bandage. The idea of a lawn is like a surgical procedure in your head, so carry three dark pails, and let this moonlight lick its lips, drum its fingers on the table, hum its little tune while sipping silver—bitter, old ventriloquist! God can't hear you. Have vespers begun? This flower has no stem, no leaves, and no petals. The lamplighter is dreaming—but of what? (I would tell you if you'd let me.)

Time to gargle. Sleep is a closed door—this dream, the crack of light underneath. Enough to breathe by, some say. Six pills. Each star hums in a different key. Torsos of flesh and an ache wrapped in barbed wire--love coiled at your feet. Preposterous. They are few, so few. You wait in the hall, you wait in the mezzanine, you wait in the whorls of a deaf god's ear. You wait.

Three dark pails and another long winter. Wash your hair. (I know you see me, and I know what you're thinking, though not what you mean. Meet me in the crisscrossing shadows, in the luminous moonlight. Kiss me while I'm sleeping.) Change your bandage. Wake the lamplighter. Tell him the lawn is whimpering. Tell him the soup is getting cold.

Poem with a Voice Like Beagles Baying

Like a Christmas ornament hanging from a schwa,
Like a package of minnows in transit to a ghost town,
Like leftovers, cold and congealed, on a virgin's dish,
Like a moon-fevered rhinestone,
Like a slag heap in an amusement park
where boys fish for carp in a muddy stream,
using their mothers' earlobes for bait,
Like rhinoplasty in a cathedral,
Like spinning tires in the gravel of philosophy,
Like a refused drink (though your thirst be antediluvian),
Like a strangled whippoorwill in a nest of semi-colons,
Like the priest's palsied hands administering the sacrament
to Venus fly-traps,
this poem, misshapen, deformed, an abomination,
a gargled aria in the bellies of frogs,
this phlegm clinging to the uvula of despair,
does it not, through its failure, its hideous visage,
its death rattle, hold humankind in greater esteem
than the silvered lies of marketers and soothsayers?

Your Poem

I know it's your poem, but I would seriously consider adding a substratum of irony, if for no other reason than to grant yourself plausible deniability.

To that end, I would have the Chinese lanterns catch fire in the pagoda scene. Think of it! All those tiny butterflies of flame dropping to the tablecloth! This could start a panic and provide a legitimate reason for Gunther and Felix to escape on the wooded path. Also, skip the business with the artichokes.

Speaking of fires, consider the train ride to Dusseldorf. I think you may be trying to accomplish too much. At the very least, hints of Gunther's employment in the wheel house should have come earlier. And where did he get the flame retardant suit? Did he carry it on board? Why do you wait till now to evoke mythological allusions to Vulcan? What role does the archeologist from Koln play?

It's your poem, but I'd omit the onomatopoeia during the love-making scene in Gunther's father's aviary. (Also, you may want to look up the definition of *deus ex machina*. I think you use it incorrectly here.)

It's your poem, but I would consider trimming the hat shopping scene. And maybe the history of smelting. Definitely the part where Felix explains his Six Theories of Numerology.

I would think about changing the point of view so that we *don't* know what the white stag is thinking. That's better left a mystery. Besides, there's a reason Second Person Omniscient is seldom used.

It's your poem, but I would add some poison mushrooms to the forest description in the final stanza. Plant them in the dark loam next to the uprooted pines, and when the moon rises, they'll look like eyes opening in the dark. And remember, no one has to eat them. It's enough to know that they're there.